The Illusion
of the End

The
Illusion
of the End

Jean Baudrillard

Translated by Chris Turner

Polity Press

This translation copyright © Polity Press 1994.
First published in France as *L'illusion de la fin* © Éditions Galilée, 1992.

Published with the assistance of the French Ministry of Culture.

First published in 1994 by Polity Press in association with Blackwell Publishers Ltd.

Reprinted 1995

Editorial office:
Polity Press
65 Bridge Street
Cambridge CB2 1UR, UK

Marketing and production:
Blackwell Publishers Ltd
108 Cowley Road
Oxford OX4 1JF, UK

ISBN 0 7456 1221 0
ISBN 0 7456 1222 9 (pbk)

A CIP catalogue record for this book is available from the British Library.

Typeset in 11 on 13pt Sabon by Photoprint, Torquay, S. Devon
Printed in Great Britain by Hartnolls Limited

This book is printed on acid-free paper.

Things can reach a state of Breakdown greater than
themselves, that is to say, they can attain a degree of
impairment at which their existence has less value than a
zero-existence, a state where replacement has become a
maleficent temptation . . .
Macedonio Fernandez

It is in the absolute void that the absolute event occurs. So
the void must only have been relative, since death has
remained virtual.

Contents

Translator's acknowledgements

Thanks are due to Leslie Hill and Marie-Dominique Maison for invaluable help with linguistic matters and to Glynis Powell for research assistance. I must also thank Jean Baudrillard for taking time from his many other commitments to respond to my queries. All the footnotes to the text are mine.

This translation is dedicated to the memory of my father, Reggie Turner (1919–94).

Pataphysics of the year 2000

A tormenting thought: as of a certain point, history was no
longer *real*. Without noticing it, all mankind suddenly left reality;
everything happening since then was supposedly not true; but we
supposedly didn't notice. Our task would now be to find that
point, and as long as we didn't have it, we would be forced to
abide in our present destruction.

Elias Canetti

Various plausible hypotheses may be advanced to explain this
vanishing of history. Canetti's expression 'all mankind suddenly
left reality' irresistibly evokes the idea of that escape velocity a
body requires to free itself from the gravitational field of a star or
planet. Staying with this image, one might suppose that the
acceleration of modernity, of technology, events and media, of all
exchanges – economic, political and sexual – has propelled us to
'escape velocity', with the result that we have flown free of the
referential sphere of the real and of history. We are 'liberated' in
every sense of the term, so liberated that we have taken leave of a
certain space-time, passed beyond a certain horizon in which the
real is possible because gravitation is still strong enough for
things to be reflected and thus in some way to endure and have
some consequence.

A degree of slowness (that is, a certain speed, but not too
much), a degree of distance, but not too much, and a degree of
liberation (an energy for rupture and change), but not too much,
are needed to bring about the kind of condensation or significant
crystallization of events we call history, the kind of coherent
unfolding of causes and effects we call reality [*le réel*].

Once beyond this gravitational effect, which keeps bodies in orbit, all the atoms of meaning get lost in space. Each atom pursues its own trajectory to infinity and is lost in space. This is precisely what we are seeing in our present-day societies, intent as they are on accelerating all bodies, messages and processes in all directions and which, with modern media, have created for every event, story and image a simulation of an infinite trajectory. Every political, historical and cultural fact possesses a kinetic energy which wrenches it from its own space and propels it into a hyperspace where, since it will never return, it loses all meaning. No need for science fiction here: already, here and now – in the shape of our computers, circuits and networks – we have the particle accelerator which has smashed the referential orbit of things once and for all.

So far as history is concerned, its telling has become impossible because that telling (*re-citatum*) is, by definition, the possible recurrence of a sequence of meanings. Now, through the impulse for total dissemination and circulation, every event is granted its own liberation; every fact becomes atomic, nuclear, and pursues its trajectory into the void. In order to be disseminated to infinity, it has to be fragmented like a particle. This is how it is able to achieve a velocity of no-return which carries it out of history once and for all. Every set of phenomena, whether cultural totality or sequence of events, has to be fragmented, disjointed, so that it can be sent down the circuits; every kind of language has to be resolved into a binary formulation so that it can circulate not, any longer, in our memories, but in the luminous, electronic memory of the computers. No human language can withstand the speed of light. No event can withstand being beamed across the whole planet. No meaning can withstand acceleration. No history can withstand the centrifugation of facts or their being short-circuited in real time (to pursue the same train of thought: no sexuality can withstand being liberated, no culture can withstand being hyped, no truth can withstand being verified, etc.).

Nor is theory in a position to 'reflect (on)' anything. It can only tear concepts from their critical zone of reference and force them beyond a point of no-return (it too is moving into the hyperspace of simulation), a process whereby it loses all 'objective' validity but gains substantially in real affinity with the present system.

The second hypothesis regarding the vanishing of history is the opposite of the first. It has to do not with processes speeding up but slowing down. It too comes directly from physics.

Matter slows the passing of time. To put it more precisely, time at the surface of a very dense body seems to be going in slow motion. The phenomenon intensifies as the density increases. The effect of this slowing down will be to increase the length of the light-wave emitted by this body as received by the observer. Beyond a certain limit, time stops and the wavelength becomes infinite. The wave no longer exists. The light goes out.

There is a clear analogy here with the slowing down of history when it rubs up against the astral body of the 'silent majorities'. Our societies are dominated by this mass process, not just in the demographic and sociological sense, but in the sense of a 'critical mass', of passing beyond a point of no-return. This is the most significant event within these societies: the emergence, in the very course of their mobilization and revolutionary process (they are all revolutionary by the standards of past centuries), of an equivalent force of inertia, of an immense indifference and the silent potency of that indifference. This inert matter of the social is not produced by a lack of exchanges, information or communication, but by the multiplication and saturation of exchanges. It is the product of the hyperdensity of cities, commodities, messages and circuits. It is the cold star of the social and, around that mass, history is also cooling. Events follow one upon another, cancelling each other out in a state of indifference. The masses, neutralized, mithridatized by information, in turn neutralize history and act as an *écran d'absorption*.* They themselves have no history, meaning, consciousness or desire. They are the potential residue of all history, meaning and desire. As they have

---

* The French is retained here, since to translate this by the English term 'dark trace screen' would be to forfeit the connection Baudrillard wishes to maintain with the idea of absorption.

---

unfurled in our modernity, all these fine things have stirred up a mysterious counter-phenomenon, and all today's political and social strategies are thrown out of gear by the failure to understand it.

This time we have the opposite situation: history, meaning and progress are no longer able to reach their escape velocity. They are no longer able to pull away from this overdense body which slows their trajectory, which slows time to the point where, right now, the perception and imagination of the future are beyond us. All social, historical and temporal transcendence is absorbed by that mass in its silent immanence. Political events already lack sufficient energy of their own to move us: so they run on like a silent film for which we bear collective irresponsibility. History comes to an end here, not for want of actors, nor for want of violence (there will always be more violence), nor for want of events (there will always be more events, thanks be to the media and the news networks!), but by deceleration, indifference and stupefaction. It is no longer able to transcend itself, to envisage its own finality, to dream of its own end; it is being buried beneath its own immediate effect, worn out in special effects, imploding into current events.

Deep down, one cannot even speak of the end of history here, since history will not have time to catch up with its own end. Its effects are accelerating, but its meaning is slowing inexorably. It will eventually come to a stop and be extinguished like light and time in the vicinity of an infinitely dense mass . . .

Humanity too had its big bang: a certain critical density, a certain concentration of people and exchanges presides over this explosion we call history, which is merely the dispersal of the dense and hieratic nuclei of previous civilizations. Today we have the reversive effect: crossing the threshold of the critical mass where populations, events and information are concerned triggers the opposite process of historical and political inertia. In the cosmic order, we do not know whether we have reached the escape velocity which would mean we are now in a definitive state of expansion (this will doubtless remain eternally uncertain). In the human order, where the perspectives are more limited, it may be that the very escape velocity of the species (the acceleration of births, technologies and exchanges over the centuries) creates an excess of mass and resistance which defeats the initial energy and takes us down an inexorable path of contraction and inertia.

Whether the universe is expanding to infinity or retracting towards an infinitely dense, infinitely small nucleus depends on its critical mass (and speculation on this is itself infinite by virtue of the possible invention of new particles). By analogy, whether our human history is evolutive or involutive perhaps depends on humanity's critical mass. Has the history, the movement, of the species reached the escape velocity required to triumph over the inertia of the mass? Are we set, like the galaxies, on a definitive course distancing us from one another at prodigious speed, or is this dispersal to infinity destined to come to an end and the human molecules to come back together by an opposite process of gravitation? Can the human mass, which increases every day, exert control over a pulsation of this kind?

There is a third hypothesis, a third analogy. We are still speaking of a point of disappearance, a vanishing point, but this time in music. I shall call this the stereophonic effect. We are all obsessed with high fidelity, with the quality of musical 'reproduction'. At the consoles of our stereos, armed with our tuners, amplifiers and speakers, we mix, adjust settings, multiply tracks in pursuit of a flawless sound. Is this still music? Where is the high fidelity threshold beyond which music disappears as such? It does not disappear for lack of music, but because it has passed this limit point; it disappears into the perfection of its materiality, into its own special effect. Beyond this point, there is neither judgement nor aesthetic pleasure. It is the ecstasy of musicality, and its end.

The disappearance of history is of the same order: here again, we have passed that limit where, by dint of the sophistication of events and information, history ceases to exist as such. Immediate high-powered broadcasting, special effects, secondary effects, fading and that famous feedback effect which is produced in acoustics by a source and a receiver being too close together and in history by an event and its dissemination being too close together and thus interfering disastrously – a short-circuit between cause and effect like that between the object and the experimenting subject in microphysics (and in the human sciences!). These are all things which cast a radical doubt on the event, just as excessive high fidelity casts radical doubt on music. Elias Canetti puts it well: beyond this point, nothing is true. It is for this reason that the *petite musique* of history also eludes our grasp today, that it vanishes into the microscopics or the stereophonics of news.

Right at the very heart of news, history threatens to disappear. At the heart of hi-fi, music threatens to disappear. At the heart of experimentation, the object of science threatens to disappear. At the heart of pornography, sexuality threatens to disappear. Everywhere we find the same stereophonic effect, the same effect of absolute proximity to the real, the same effect of simulation.

By definition, this vanishing point, this point short of which history *existed* and music *existed*, cannot be pinned down. Where must stereo perfection end? The boundaries are constantly being pushed back because it is technical obsession which redraws them. Where must news reporting end? One can only counter this fascination with 'real time' – the equivalent of high fidelity – with a moral objection, and there is not much point in that.

The passing of this point is thus an irreversible act, contrary to what Canetti seems to hope. We shall never get back to pre-stereo music (except by an additional technical simulation effect); we shall never get back to pre-news and pre-media history. The original essence of music, the original concept of history have disappeared because we shall never again be able to isolate them from their model of perfection which is at the same time their model of simulation, the model of their enforced assumption into a hyper-reality which cancels them out. We shall never again know what the social or music were before being exacerbated into their present useless perfection. We shall never again know what history was before its exacerbation into the technical perfection of news: we shall never again know what anything was before disappearing into the fulfilment of its model.

So, with this, the situation becomes novel once again. The fact that we are leaving history to move into the realm of simulation is merely a consequence of the fact that history itself has always, deep down, been an immense simulation model. Not in the sense that it could be said only to have existed in the narrative made of it or the interpretation given, but with regard to the time in which it unfolds – that linear time which is at once the time of an ending and of the unlimited suspending of the end. The only kind of time in which a history can take place, if, by history, we understand a succession of non-meaningless facts, each engendering the other by cause and effect, but doing so without any absolute necessity and all standing open to the future, unevenly poised. So different from time in ritual societies where the end of everything is in its beginning and ceremony retraces the perfection of that original event. In contrast to this *fulfilled* order of time, the liberation of the 'real' time of history, the production of a linear, deferred time may seem a purely artificial process. Where does this suspense come from? Where do we get the idea that what must be accomplished (Last Judgement, salvation or catastrophe) must come at the end of time and match up with some incalculable appointed term or other? This model of linearity must have seemed entirely fictitious, wholly absurd and abstract to cultures which had no sense of a deferred day of reckoning, a successive concatenation of events and a final goal. And it was, indeed, a scenario which had some difficulty establishing itself. There was fierce resistance in the early years of Christianity to the postpone-ment of the coming of God's Kingdom. The acceptance of this 'historical' perspective of salvation, that is, of its remaining unaccomplished in the immediate present, was not achieved without violence, and all the heresies would later take up this leitmotif of the immediate fulfilment of the promise in what was akin to a defiance of time. Entire communities even resorted to suicide to hasten the coming of the Kingdom. Since this latter was promised at the end of time, it seemed to them that they had only to put an end to time right away.

The whole of history has had a millennial (millenarian) challenge to its temporality running through it. In opposition to the historical perspective, which continually shifts the stakes on to a hypothetical end, there has always been a fatal exigency, a fatal strategy of time which wants to shoot straight ahead to a point beyond the end. It cannot be said that either of these tendencies has really won out, and the question 'to wait or not to wait?' has remained, throughout history, a burning issue. Since the messianic convulsion of the earliest Christians, reaching back beyond the heresies and revolts, there has always been this desire to anticipate the end, possibly by death, by a kind of seductive suicide aiming to turn God from history and make him face up to his responsibilities, those which lie beyond the end, those of the final fulfilment. And what, indeed, is terrorism, if not this effort to conjure up, in its own way, the end of history? It attempts to entrap the powers that be by an immediate, total act. Without awaiting the final term of the process, it sets itself at the ecstatic end-point, hoping to bring about the conditions for the Last Judgement. An illusory challenge, of course, but one which always fascinates, since, deep down, neither time nor history has ever been accepted. Everyone remains aware of the arbitrariness, the artificial character of time and history. And we are never fooled by those who call on us to hope.

And, terrorism apart, is there not also a hint of this parousic exigency in the global fantasy of catastrophe that hovers over today's world? A demand for a violent resolution of reality, when this latter eludes our grasp in an endless hyper-reality? For hyper-reality rules out the very occurrence of the Last Judgement or the Apocalypse or the Revolution. All the ends we have envisaged elude our grasp and history has no chance of bringing them about, since it will, in the interim, have come to an end (it's always the story of Kafka's Messiah: he arrives too late, a day too late, and the time-lag is unbearable). So one might as well short-circuit the Messiah, bring forward the end. This has always been the demonic temptation: to falsify ends and the calculation of ends, to falsify time and the occurrence of things, to hurry them along, impatient to see them accomplished, or secretly sensing that the promise of accomplishment is itself also false and diabolical.

Even our obsession with 'real time', with the instantaneity of news, has a secret millenarianism about it: cancelling the flow of time, cancelling delay, suppressing the sense that the event is happening elsewhere, anticipating its end by freeing ourselves from linear time, laying hold of things almost before they have taken place. In this sense, 'real time' is something even more artificial than a recording, and is, at the same time, its denial – if we want immediate enjoyment of the event, if we want to experience it at the instant of its occurrence, as if we were there, this is because we no longer have any confidence in the meaning or purpose of the event. The same denial is found in apparently opposite behaviour – recording, filing and memorizing everything of our own past and the past of all cultures. Is this not a symptom of a collective presentiment of the end, a sign that events and the living time of history have had their day and that we have to arm ourselves with the whole battery of artificial memory, all the signs of the past, to face up to the absence of a future and the glacial times which await us? Are not mental and intellectual structures currently going underground, burying themselves in memories, in archives, in search of an improbable resurrection? All thoughts are going underground in cautious anticipation of the year 2000. They can already scent the terror of the year 2000. They are instinctively adopting the solution of those cryogenized individuals plunged into liquid nitrogen until the means can be found to enable them to survive.

These societies, these generations which no longer expect anything from some future 'coming', and have less and less confidence in history, which dig in behind their futuristic technologies, behind their stores of information and inside the beehive networks of communication where time is at last wiped out by pure circulation, will perhaps never reawaken. But they do not know that. The year 2000 will not perhaps take place. But they do not know that.

The reversal of history

At some point in the 1980s, history took a turn in the opposite direction. Once the apogee of time, the summit of the curve of evolution, the solstice of history had been passed, the downward slope of events began and things began to run in reverse. It seems that, like cosmic space, historical space-time is also curved. By the same chaotic effect in time as in space, things go quicker and quicker as they approach their term, just as water mysteriously accelerates as it approaches a waterfall.

In the Euclidean space of history, the shortest path between two points is the straight line, the line of Progress and Democracy. But this is only true of the linear space of the Enlightenment. In our non-Euclidean *fin de siècle* space, a baleful curvature unfailingly deflects all trajectories. This is doubtless linked to the sphericity of time (visible on the horizon of the end of the century, just as the earth's sphericity is visible on the horizon at the end of the day) or the subtle distortion of the gravitational field.

Ségalen says that once the Earth has become a sphere, every movement distancing us from a point by the same token also begins to bring us closer to that point. This is true of time as well. Each apparent movement of history brings us imperceptibly closer to its antipodal point, if not indeed to its starting point. This is the end of linearity. In this perspective, the future no longer exists. But if there is no longer a future, there is no longer an end either. *So this is not even the end of history.* We are faced with a paradoxical process of reversal, a reversive effect of modernity which, having reached its speculative limit and extrapolated all its virtual developments, is disintegrating into its simple elements in a catastrophic process of recurrence and turbulence.

By this retroversion of history to infinity, this hyperbolic curvature, the century itself is escaping its end. By this retroaction of events, we are eluding our own deaths. Metaphorically, then, we shall not even reach the symbolic term of the end, the symbolic term of the year 2000.

Can one escape this curving back of history which causes it to retrace its own steps and obliterate its own tracks, escape this fatal asymptote which causes us, as it were, to rewind modernity like a tape? We are so used to playing back every film – the fictional ones and the films of our lives – so contaminated by the technology of retrospection, that we are quite capable, in our present dizzy spin, of running history over again like a film played backwards.

Are we condemned, in the vain hope of not abiding in our present destruction, as Canetti has it, to the retrospective melancholia of living everything through again in order to correct it all, in order to elucidate it all (it is almost as though psychoanalysis were spreading its shadow over the whole of our history: when the same events, the same conjunctures are reproduced in almost the same terms, when the same wars break out between the same peoples, and all that had passed and gone re-emerges as though driven by an irrepressible phantasm, one might almost see this as the work of a form of primary process or unconscious), do we have to summon all past events to appear before us, to reinvestigate it all as though we were conducting a trial? A mania for trials has taken hold of us in recent times, together with a mania for responsibility, precisely at the point when this latter is becoming increasingly hard to pin down. We are looking to remake a clean history, to whitewash all the

abominations: the obscure (resentful) feeling behind the proliferation of scandals is that history itself is a scandal. A
retroprocess which may drag us into a mania for origins, going
back even beyond history, back to the conviviality of animal
existence, to the primitive biotope, as can already be seen in the
ecologists' flirtation with an impossible origin.

The only way of escaping this, of breaking with this recession
and obsession, would seem to be to set ourselves, from the outset,
on a different temporal orbit, to leapfrog our shadows, leapfrog
the shadow of the century, to take an elliptical short-cut and pass
beyond the end, not allowing it time to take place. The advantage
is that we would at least preserve what remains of history, instead
of subjecting it to an agonizing revision, and deliver it up to those
who will carry out the post-mortem on its corpse, as one carries
out a post-mortem on one's childhood in an interminable
analysis. This would at least mean conserving its memory and its
glory, whereas currently, in the guise of revision and rehabilitation, we are cancelling out one by one all the events which have
preceded us by obliging them to repent.

If we could escape this end-of-century moratorium, with its
deferred day of reckoning, which looks curiously like a work of
mourning – a *failed* one – and which consists in reviewing
everything, rewriting everything, restoring everything, face-lifting
everything, to produce, as it seems, in a burst of paranoia a
perfect set of accounts at the end of the century, a universally
positive balance sheet (the reign of human rights over the whole
planet, democracy everywhere, the definitive obliteration of all
conflict and, if possible, the obliteration of all 'negative' events
from our memories), if we could escape this international
cleaning and polishing effort in which all the nations of the world
can be seen vying today, if we could spare ourselves this
democratic extreme unction by which the New World Order is
heralded, we would at least allow the events which have preceded
us to retain their glory, character, meaning and singularity.
Whereas we seem in such a hurry to cover up the worst before the
bankruptcy proceedings start (everyone is secretly afraid of the
terrifying balance sheet we are going to present in the year 2000)

that there will be nothing left of our history at the end of the millennium, nothing of its illumination, of the violence of its events. If there is something distinctive about an event — about what constitutes an event and thus has historical value — it is the fact that it is irreversible, that there is always something in it which exceeds meaning and interpretation. But it is precisely the opposite we are seeing today: all that has happened this century in terms of progress, liberation, revolution and violence is about to be revised for the better.

This is the problem: is the course of modernity reversible, and is that reversal itself irreversible? How far can this retrospective form go, this end-of-millennium dream? Is there not a 'history barrier', analogous to the sound or speed barrier, beyond which, in its palinodical movement, it could not pass?

The ascent of the vacuum towards the periphery

On the eve of the 1990s, in the midst of some unexpected events and with an eye to others just as unpredictable, there formed, among a number of friends, the idea of an agency which would itself be invisible, anonymous and clandestine: the Stealth Agency. This could equally well be called:

ANATHEMATIC ILLIMITED
TRANSFATAL EXPRESS
VIRAL INCORPORATED
INTERNATIONAL EPIDEMICS*

As an agency for gathering news of unreal events in order to disinform the public of them, it remained, itself, unreal. It thus fulfilled its role perfectly, eluding all radar screens – a formula unique and forever virtual.

Implied in this Agency was the point that there are no longer any ideas grappling with facts – that was the 'Utopia' of the 1960s and 1970s – no longer really any actors grappling with events, nor intellectuals grappling with their meaning, but a storm

* All the terms in capitals are in English in the original.

of events of no importance, without either real actors or authorized interpreters: *actio* has disappeared at the same moment as *auctoritas*. All that remains is *actualité*, 'action' in the cinematographic sense, and 'auction', the selling-off of the event on the overheated news market. The event captured not, as it used to be, in action, but in speculation and chain reactions spinning off towards the extremes of a facticity with which interpretation can no longer keep pace.

Simulation is precisely this irresistible unfolding, this sequencing of things as though they had a meaning, when they are governed only by artificial *montage* and non-meaning. Putting the event up for auction by radical disinformation. Setting a price on the event, as against setting it in play, setting it in history. If there are any historical stakes, they remain secret, enigmatic; they are resolved in events which do not really take place. And I am not referring here to ordinary events, but to the events of Eastern Europe, the Gulf War, etc. Now, the aim of the Agency was precisely to set up against this simulation a radical desimulation or, in other words, *to lift the veil on the fact of events not taking place.* And thus to make itself secret and enigmatic in their image, to get through to a certain void, a certain non-meaning, by contrast with the media, which are frantic to plug up all the gaps. To move within the void of events like Chuang Tzu's butcher in the interstitial void of the body.* Admittedly, this kind of sly, surreptitious intervention on the side of the void against the grotesque, Ubuesque infatuation with news and the political scene was merely a dream and, by dint of being secret and enigmatic, no more came into being, in the end, than did the events themselves. It fell into the same black hole, the same virtual space, as the non-events of which it was to speak (secretly, unbeknown to everyone, while remaining operational, exactly like these new-style events which are only events to the extent that they are

---

* In English translations of Chuang Tzu (Zhuang Zi), this figure is often identified as a 'cook'. Thomas Merton's translation contains the following lines: 'Guided by natural line,/By the secret opening, the hidden space,/My cleaver finds its own way./I cut through no joint, chop no bone' (*The Way of Chuang Tzu*, London: Unwin, 1970, p. 46).

media events). An apparently irresolvable paradox. But the idea is not dead.

The Stealth Agency chimed in with events being on strike, with history being on strike. Like history, it was a consumer of absent events, attempting to give the most precise non-information about that absence of events, that indefinite sit-in strike in which history – the empty space over which the spectres of Power still hover – was occupied, just as workers might occupy a factory – that empty space of Labour, over which the spectre of Capital still hovers.

It is as though events passed on the strike call to each other. One after the other they deserted their time, transforming it into an empty *actualité* where only the visual psychodrama of news was left to unfold. And this event strike led to history being locked out. The fact that it is no longer the event that generates news, but the reverse, has incalculable consequences, as the whole *travail du négatif* disappears on the horizon of the media, exactly as work disappears on the horizon of capital. Here again, the relations are inverted: it is no longer work that serves the reproduction of capital, but capital which produces and reproduces work. A gigantic parody of the relations of production.

This disruption of cause and effect is not now the work of the critical consciousness, but of objective irony alone. Thus it was the Agency's duty not only to avoid the temptation of providing information on the events which had 'downed tools', but also to avoid appending a critical commentary to them, in order to capture the originality of this non-event, which is the originality of an objective irony. For the radical irony of our history is that things no longer really take place, while nonetheless seeming to. This is the opposite of the traditional ruse of history which brought about changes that were crucial but did not appear to be so.

When you think that we took the events in Eastern Europe at face value, with their good, sound coin of freedom and 'democratic values', and the Gulf War, with its Human Rights and New World Order! These events were auctioned off well above their value. The historical scene today is like the art market. Against this speculative inflation, which leaves everyone on edge – that is, both overexcited and indifferent, riveted and apathetic – against these *gidouille* events, worthy of the *Grande Gidouille* of History,* we had to find an ironic form of the disruption of information, a casual form of writing to match the casual *événementialité* of our age, together with a subtly catastrophic form which fits with the coming of the end of the century. We had to find, in this event strike, the thread running through, which is that of deterrence, the baleful form which presides over the nullity of our age.

Deterrence is a very peculiar form of action: it is *what causes something not to take place*. It dominates the whole of our contemporary period, which tends not so much to produce events as to cause something not to occur, while looking as though it is a historical event. Or else events do take place in the stead of some other event which did not. War, history, reality and passion – deterrence plays its part in all these. It causes strange events to take place(!), events which do not in any way advance history, but rather run it backwards, back along the opposite slope, unintelligible to our historical sense (only things which move in the direction of history [*le sens de l'histoire*] have historical meaning [*sens historique*]), events which no longer have a negative (progressive, critical or revolutionary) potency since *their only negativity is in the fact of their not taking place*. Disturbing.

The hold deterrence has on us even extends to the past. It can remove all certainty about facts and evidence. It can destabilize memory just as it destabilizes prediction. It is a diabolical force which wrecks the actual acting out of events or, if they still take place – if they have taken place – destroys their credibility.

Perhaps this curvature of things which deprives them of meaning or linear end is merely a depression in the meteorologi-

---

* The *gidouille* here is the great belly or paunch of Jarry's Père Ubu, which has acquired a broader sense in French 'pataphysical' usage. On its origins and signification, see, for example, Keith Beaumont, *Alfred Jarry: A Critical and Biographical Study*, Leicester: Leicester University Press, 1984.

cal sense of the term – the emptiness we feel being the effect not of a failing of meaning or memory, but of a strange attraction coming from elsewhere. Perhaps the atony, the catatonia we are experiencing is to be interpreted in the opposite sense, not as a void left by the ebbing of past events, but a void due to the suction effect of a future event, to the anticipatory sucking up by a nearby mass of all the oxygen we breathe, creating a violent depressurizing of the social, political, cultural and mental sphere.

A pataphysical hypothesis, that of anti-gravity, anti-density – of a science of imaginary solutions rising above physics and metaphysics. In his *Exploits and Opinions of Dr Faustroll*, Jarry sketches the contours of this strange attraction, brought about by overturning the principles of physics: 'Current science is based on the principle of induction: most people have seen a certain phenomenon most often precede or follow some other phenomenon and conclude therefrom that this will always be the case . . . But, instead of formulating the law of the fall of a body towards a centre, why not give preference to that of the ascent of a vacuum towards a periphery, the vacuum being considered a unit of non-density, a hypothesis far less arbitrary than the choice of a concrete unit of positive density.'

Inverse attraction by the void, rather than attraction of solids by other solids. Perhaps it is this which gives our events this particular coloration, this flavour (or, rather, insipidity) of emptiness, this inanity. Even as they occur, they might already be 'vanishing events' – of little meaning because already heading towards the void. Running counter to the old physics of meaning would be a new gravitation – the true, the only gravitation: attraction by the void. Doubtless the most basic of natural laws.

This would explain quite a number of anomalies, including those in the realms of the mind and the 'psychological' field. So, our forms of action and mobility are not so much a matter of positive drives as of expulsion and repulsion. The centrifugal mobility of particles seeking to escape from density and join up with what? A mysterious periphery of space, an anti-gravity. Thus it would be possible to escape from the heavy form, the gravity of 'desire', conceived as positive attraction, by the much more subtle eccentricity of seduction, which would be, to take up again some old cosmogonies that were not without their charm, the last-gasp escape from the body of molecules that are much too light and know only one line of flight – towards the void (so it is with poetic language, where each particle finds its resolution in anagrammatical resonance).

We may say of the new events that they hollow out before them the void into which they plunge. They are intent, it seems, on one thing alone – being forgotten. They leave hardly any scope for interpretation, except for all interpretations at once, by which they evade any desire to give them meaning and elude the heavy attraction of a continuous history to enter upon the light orbit of a discontinuous one. They arrive – mostly unforeseen – more quickly than their shadows, but they have no sequel. Meteoric events, of the same chaotic inconsequence as cloud formations. So, with the events of Eastern Europe, for example, we have the impression of a long negative accumulation and a sudden resolution, like the obvious, instant conclusion to operations which elude our understanding. In these conditions, such events, which are nonetheless important, have the strange aftertaste of something that has already happened before, something unfolding retrospectively – an aftertaste which does not bode well for a meaningful future. Our only surprise is that we were not able to foresee them and our only regret that we do not know how to draw any consequences from them. The screen of history fluctuates at the same irregular rhythm as natural phenomena.

One has the impression that events form all on their own and drift unpredictably towards their vanishing point – the peripheral void of the media. Just as physicists now see their particles only as a trajectory on a screen, we no longer have the pulsing of events, but only the cardiogram, have neither representation nor recollection of them, but merely the (flat) encephalogram, neither desire nor enjoyment of them, but only the psychodrama and the TV image.

It is a bit like *in vitro* procreation: the embryo of the real event is transferred into the artificial womb of the news media, there to give birth to many orphaned foetuses which have neither fathers nor mothers. The event is entitled to the same procreative practices as birth and the same euthanasian practices as death.

It is to this perhaps that we owe this 'fun physics' effect: the impression that events, collective or individual, have been bundled into a memory hole. This blackout is due, no doubt, to this movement of reversal, this parabolic curvature of historical space. For the past can only be represented and reflected if it pushes us in the other direction, towards a future of some kind. Retrospection is dependent on a prospection which enables us to refer to something as past and gone, and thus as having really taken place. If, by some strange revolution, we set off in the opposite direction and turn inwards into this dimension of the past, then we can no longer represent that something to ourselves. The beam of memory bends, and makes every event a black hole. We experience this subjectively too, in the sudden loss of our memories, the break in the continuity of names, faces and familiar forms. In this kind of catastrophic memory failure, there is neither natural forgetting nor unconscious repression. It is the inversion of the temporal field of gravity which means that the signs of the past no longer have sufficient specific mass, sufficient nuclear mass to hold them, nor the mirror of the present enough to reflect them. The memory gaps are a little bit like the holes in the ozone layer, the holes into which our protective screen is breaking up. But perhaps they are not big enough for what falls into them to begin to spin, releasing the light particles from the heavy, widening and deepening the black hole through which the dead bodies will release their ethereal substance, as in Dante or Giordano Bruno. It is in the absolute void that the absolute event occurs. So the void must only have been relative, since death has remained virtual.

The event strike

What has been lost is the glory of the event, what Benjamin would term its aura. For centuries, the keynote of history was glory, a very powerful illusion and one which played on the everlasting nature of time, in that it was inherited from one's ancestors and would be handed on to one's descendants. That passion seems laughable today. Whereas, in the past, the aim was to lose oneself in something prodigious, to achieve the 'immortality' Hannah Arendt speaks of, which had a transcendence equal to that of God (glory and salvation long contended for the souls of men, like passion and compassion, those rivals before the Eternal), what we seek now is not glory but identity, not an illusion but, on the contrary, an accumulation of proofs – anything that can serve as evidence of a historical existence.

The prodigious event, the event which is measured neither by its causes nor its consequences but creates its own stage and its own dramatic effect, no longer exists. History has gradually narrowed down to the field of its probable causes and effects, and, even more recently, to the field of current events – its effects 'in real time'. Events now have no more significance than their anticipated meaning, their programming and their broadcasting. Only *this event strike* constitutes a true historical phenomenon – this refusal to signify anything whatever, or this capacity to signify anything at all. This is the true end of history, the end of historical Reason.

But it would be too much to hope that we had finished with history. For it is possible not only that history has disappeared (the *travail du négatif*, political reason, the prestige of the event have all gone), but also that we still have to *fuel its end*. It is entirely as though we were still continuing to manufacture history, whereas, in accumulating the signs of the social, the signs of the political, the signs of progress and change, we are merely feeding the end of history. While history, cannibalistic and necrophagous, constantly calls for new victims, for new events, so as to be done with them a little bit more. Socialism is a fine example of this. It is to socialism that it will have fallen, by the collapse of the historical reason it claimed to embody, to manage the end of history, to fuel the end.

We used to ask what might come after the orgy – mourning or melancholia? Doubtless neither, but an interminable clean-up of all the vicissitudes of modern history and its processes of liberation (of peoples, sex, dreams, art and the unconscious – in short, of all that makes up the orgy of our times), in an atmosphere dominated by the apocalyptic presentiment that all this is coming to an end. Rather than pressing forward and taking flight into the future, we prefer the retrospective apocalypse, and a blanket revisionism. Our societies have all become revisionistic: they are quietly rethinking everything, laundering their political crimes, their scandals, licking their wounds, fuelling their ends. Celebration and commemoration are themselves merely the soft form of necrophagous cannibalism, the homeopathic form of murder by easy stages. This is the work of the heirs, whose *ressentiment* towards the deceased is boundless. Museums, jubilees, festivals, complete works, the publication of the tiniest of unpublished fragments – all this shows that we are entering an active age of *ressentiment* and repentance.

Acts of glorification and commemoration clearly form part of this collective flagellation. We are particularly well served in France: our public life has been overtaken by a veritable ritual of

mourning and condolence. And all our monuments are mauso-
leums: the Pyramid, the Arch at La Défense, the Musée d'Orsay,
that fine Pharaonic chamber, the new National Library, cenotaph
of culture. Not counting the Revolution, which is a monument in
itself, the bicentenary of which was the finest simulation of an
event to be seen at the end of the century.

There are two forms of forgetting: on the one hand, the slow or
violent extermination of memory, on the other, the spectacular
promotion of a phenomenon, shifting it from historical space into
the sphere of advertising, the media becoming the site of a
temporal strategy of prestige . . . This is how we have manufactured for ourselves, with great swathes of promotional images,
a synthetic memory which serves as our primal reference, our
founding myth, and which, most importantly, absolves us of the
real event of Revolution.

'Revolution is not on the agenda in France because the Great
Revolution occurred and has served as an example for all others
over two centuries . . . Our entire aim in present-day France is to
ensure that there will be no revolution' (Louis Mermaz). This is
how it is: it happened, it is finished, it will never happen again.
The whole of our system is based on this negative anticipation.
Not only are we no longer able to produce a new history, we are
not even able to ensure its symbolic reproduction. We build an
opera house at the Bastille. A laughable rehabilitation: royal
music is to be served up there to the people. Yet it is not the
people who will benefit. It is the cultural elite who will go there,
confirming the rule that the privileged are happy to hallow with
art and pleasure the places where others died.

Might one suggest to the people that they storm the opera
house and tear it down on the symbolic date of 14 July? Might
one suggest that they parade the bloody heads of our modern
cultural governors on the end of pikestaffs?

But we no longer make history. We have become reconciled
with it and protect it like an endangered masterpiece. Times have
changed. We have today a perfectly pious *vision* of the Revolution, cast in terms of the Rights of Man. Not even a nostalgic
vision, but one recycled in the terms of post-modern intellectual

comfort. A vision which allows us to eliminate Saint-Just from the *Dictionnaire de la Révolution*. 'Overrated rhetoric', says François Furet, perfect historian of the repentance of the Terror and of glory.

There are those who let the dead bury their dead, and there are those who are forever digging them up to finish them off. Having failed both in their symbolic murder and their work of mourning, it is not enough for them that others should be dead; they have to disinter them once again to impale them – this is the Carpentras complex (after the Timişoara complex: the faking of corpses for TV), the desecration complex.

Nothing lends itself so well to this operation as the centenary of a death. With Rimbaud, Van Gogh and Nietzsche, 1991 will have been exceptional in terms of vile acts of desecration.

One can see a kind of suicidal behaviour in this compulsion on the part of the cultural and intellectual elite to exalt thinkers who have only scorn for that elite and are its living condemnation: Céline, Artaud, Bataille, Nietzsche. Might this be a product of one of those failures of instinct which the last-mentioned diagnosed more than a century ago – a failure which character-izes a species doomed by its inability to judge what is good for it? If the left were a species, and culture obeyed the laws of natural selection, it would have disappeared long ago. Flirting with what is implacably opposed to it, dying from a total contradiction between its critical thinking and its action, attempting to reconcile its critical subconscious and its presence in power by turning culture into a mode of government. These things are all part and parcel, already, of the forms of repentance.

It isn't just terrorists who repent. Intellectuals showed them the way, the Sartreans and others having been in the van of repentance from the 1950s onwards. Today, the whole century is repenting, class (or race) repentance everywhere predominating over class pride and consciousness. It is the sign that the century is becoming intellectualized. It is becoming intellectual today just as it became bourgeois a century ago. And the term 'intellectual' will one day disappear, just as the word 'bourgeois' – which now exposes only the person who uses it to ridicule – has disappeared.

The auto-dissolution common to both West and East is visible in the deterioration of the structures of power and representation (thus, the more the political sphere becomes intellectualized, the more it secretly denies its own will to govern, and this *ressentiment* towards itself is the source of all corruption). But it can also be seen in the multiple strategies for re-enchanting values, cultures and differences. We expend all the energy of that dissolution in resisting our own end, which we can then neither enjoy nor be engulfed by. A gigantic night of the fourth of August* would be preferable, a great night of the Rights of Man, on which the whole of humanity would renounce those rights as the aristocrats once renounced their privileges, and the renunciation would take on excessive dimensions. What can occur to rescue us from endlessly trawling over our own culture?

It seems we are condemned to the infinite retrospective of all that has preceded us. What is true of politics and morality seems true of art also. The whole drift of painting has withdrawn from the future and shifted towards the past. Present-day art is currently reappropriating the works of the – distant, recent or even contemporary – past. This is what Russell Connor calls the 'abduction of modern art'.† Now, admittedly, this reappropriation is supposed to be ironic. But the humour here is merely the transparent invocation of humour. Like the worn threads of a piece of fabric, it is an irony produced only by the disillusion of things, a fossilized irony. The little trick of placing the nude from Manet's *Déjeuner sur l'herbe* opposite Cézanne's *Card Players*, as one might put an admiral's hat on a monkey, is nothing more than the advertising-style irony currently engulfing the world of art. It is the irony of repentance and *ressentiment* towards one's

---

* A reference to the date in 1789 on which the nobles gave up their feudal rights. Not only was this in itself, as Simon Schama remarks, 'a bonfire of particularisms', it also ushered in what he describes as 'a cult of self-dispossession' (*Citizens*, London, 1989, p. 439).

† This expression has been retranslated from the French exhibition catalogue in which the author encountered it.

own culture. No doubt repentance and *ressentiment* constitute the last stage of the history of art, just as, according to Nietzsche, they constitute the last stage of the genealogy of morals. It is a parody, or rather a palinode, of art and the history of art (a development reflecting that of history *tout court*) – a parody of culture by culture itself as an act of vengeance, characteristic of radical disillusionment. It is as though history were rifling through its own dustbins and looking for redemption in the rubbish.

The end of history is, alas, also the end of the dustbins of history. There are no longer any dustbins even for disposing of old ideologies, old regimes, old values. Where are we going to throw Marxism, which actually invented the dustbins of history? (Yet, there is some justice here since the very people who invented them have fallen in.) Conclusion: if there are no more dustbins of history, *this is because History itself has become a dustbin*. It has become its own dustbin. Just as the planet itself is becoming its own dustbin.

When ice freezes, all the excrement rises to the surface. And so, when the dialectic was frozen, all the sacred excrement of the dialectic came to the surface. When the future is deep-frozen – and, indeed, even the present – we see all the excrement come up from the past.

The problem then becomes one of waste. It is not just material substances, including nuclear ones, which pose a waste problem but also the defunct ideologies, bygone utopias, dead concepts and fossilized ideas which continue to pollute our mental space. Historical and intellectual refuse pose an even more serious problem than industrial waste. Who will rid us of the sedimentation of centuries of stupidity? As for history – that living lump of waste, that dying monster which, like the corpse in Ionesco,* continues to swell after it has died – how are we to be rid of it?

The ecological imperative is that all wastes must be recycled. Otherwise, they will circle endlessly like satellites around the

* A reference to Ionesco's *Amédée, ou comment s'en débarrasser.*

earth, which has itself returned to the state of a lump of cosmic waste. What is happening with history is the foreshadowing of this dilemma: we can either perish under the weight of the non-degradable waste of the great empires, the grand narratives, the great systems made obsolete by their own gigantism, or else recycle all this waste in the synthetic form of a heteroclite history, as we are doing today in the name of Democracy and Human Rights, which are never anything but the confused end-product of the reprocessing of all the residues of history – crusher residues in which all the ethnic, linguistic, feudal and ideological phantoms of earlier societies float. Amnesia, anamnesis, the anachronistic revival of all the figures of the past – royalty, feudalism. Though did they ever really disappear? Democracy itself (a proliferating form, the lowest common denominator of all our liberal societies), this planetary democracy of the Rights of Man, is to real freedom what Disneyland is to the imaginary. In relation to the modern demand for freedom, it offers the same characteristics as recycled paper.

There is in fact no insoluble waste problem. The problem is resolved by the post-modern invention of recycling and the incinerator. The Great Incinerators of history, from whose ashes the Phoenix of post-modernity is resuscitated! We have to come to terms with the idea that everything that was not degradable or exterminable is today recyclable, and hence that there is no final solution. We shall not be spared the worst – that is, *History will not come to an end* – since the leftovers, all the leftovers – the Church, communism, ethnic groups, conflicts, ideologies – are indefinitely recyclable. What is stupendous is that nothing one thought superseded by history has really disappeared. All the archaic, anachronistic forms are there ready to re-emerge, intact and timeless, like the viruses deep in the body. History has only wrenched itself from cyclical time to fall into the order of the recyclable.

The thawing of the East

Hooray, history is back from the dead!

The great event of the end of the century is under way. Everyone can breathe again at the idea that history, stifled for a time in the grip of totalitarian ideology, is resuming its course with renewed vigour now that the blockade on the countries of Eastern Europe has been lifted. The field of history is at last opened up again to the unpredictable bustle of peoples and their thirst for freedom. In contrast to the depressive mythology which generally accompanies the ends of centuries, it seems this one is to usher in a new and illustrious resurgence of the final process, to bring fresh hope and a revival of all historical challenges. Away with all those evil auguries of the end of history. How can its reality and vitality be doubted when such events are taking place before our eyes?

Seen at closer quarters, the event is a bit more mysterious, and might with much greater accuracy be described as an unidentified 'historical' object. This thawing of the Eastern bloc, this thawing of liberty is certainly an extraordinary turn of events. But what becomes of liberty when it is defrosted? The operation is a perilous one and its outcome uncertain (even leaving aside the fact that what has been defrosted cannot be deep-frozen again). The USSR and the Eastern bloc have not just served as a deep-freeze for freedom; they have also provided a testing ground, an

THE THAWING OF THE EAST

experimental environment in which it was isolated and subjected
to very high pressures. The West, for its part, is little more than a
repository or, more accurately, a dumping ground for freedom
and human rights. If ultra-freezing was the distinctive – and
negative – mark of the Eastern world, the ultra-fluidity of our
Western world is even more disreputable since, as a consequence
of the liberation and liberalization of mores and opinions, the
problem of liberty quite simply cannot be posed here any longer.
It is virtually over and done with. In the West, freedom – the Idea
of Freedom – has died a natural death: this we have seen in all the
recent commemorations. In the East it was murdered, but there is
no such thing as the perfect crime. It will be very interesting, from
an experimental point of view, to see what freedom is like when it
resurfaces, when it is resuscitated after all sign of it had been
blotted out. We shall see what a process of reanimation or *post-
mortem* rehabilitation looks like. Perhaps defrosted liberty is not
so attractive as all that. And what if it turned out to be intent on
just one thing: bartering itself off in a binge of cars and electrical
goods, not to mention mind-bending drugs and pornography;
that is, immediately trading itself off against Western liquid
assets, switching over from an end of history by deep-freezing to
an end of history by ultra-fluidity and circulation? Because the
enthralling thing about these events in Eastern Europe is not to
see them meekly coming to the aid of an ailing democracy by
bringing it fresh energy (and new markets), but to see the
telescoping of two specific patterns of the end of history: the one
where it ends deep-frozen in the concentration camps and the
other where, by contrast, it ends in the total, centrifugal
expansion of communication. In each case, it is a final solution.
And it may be that the thawing of human rights is the socialist
equivalent of the 'depressurizing of the West': a mere discharge
into the Western void of the energies trapped for half a century in
the East.

The fervour surrounding events can be deceptive: if that of the
Eastern bloc countries is merely an ardent desire to be free of
ideology, merely a fervent desire to imitate the free-market

countries, where all liberty has already been exchanged for technological ease of living, then we shall see once and for all what freedom is worth and know it cannot perhaps ever be regained. History serves up no second helpings. On the other hand – and this is the unpredictable part for us, for the West (after all, when the Evil Empire collapses Good cannot remain exactly as it was before!) – this thaw in the East may be as harmful in the long term as the excess of carbon gases in the upper layers of the atmosphere, creating a political greenhouse effect and such a warming of human relations on the planet, with the melting of the communist ice-floes, that the shores of the West will be flooded. Curiously, whereas we dread the climatic melting of ice-floes and see it as representing a potential catastrophe, as democrats, we long with all our might for such a thaw on the political front.

If, in the old days, the USSR had dumped its stock of gold on the world market, that market would have been completely destabilized. If the Eastern bloc countries were to put back into circulation the vast stock of freedom they have been keeping on ice, they would similarly destabilize the very fragile metabolism of Western values, which requires that freedom no longer manifest itself as action but as a virtual and consensual form of interaction, not as drama, but as the universal psychodrama of liberalism. A sudden injection of freedom as a lived relationship – as violent and active transcendence, as Idea – would be catastrophic in every way for our air-conditioned redistribution of values. Yet this is what we are asking of those in the East: the idea of freedom in exchange for the material signs of freedom. A perfectly diabolical pact, in which one side is in danger of losing its soul, the other its comfort.

The masked societies (the communist societies) are now unmasked. What face do they present? We shed our masks long ago and it is a long time since we had either masks or faces. We have no memory either. We have reached the point of seeking in water a memory without traces, of hoping (I here crave Benveniste's indulgence) that something still remains when even the molecular traces have disappeared.* It is the same with our freedom: we would be hard pressed to produce any sign of it and we have reached the point of postulating its infinitesimal, impalpable, undetectable existence in a milieu of such high (programmatic, operational) dilution that only its spectre still hovers across our memories.

The wellspring of freedom has run so dry in the West (as witness the commemoration of the French Revolution) that we must place all our hopes in the East European deposits that have at last been uncovered and opened up. But once this stock of liberty has been released (the Idea of Liberty having become as scarce as a natural resource), what can ensue but, as on any market, an intense, superficial burst of trading, followed by a rapid collapse of differential energies and asset values.

What is the meaning of *glasnost*? The retrospective transparency of all the signs of modernity, speeded up and second-hand (it is almost a post-modern remake of our original version of modernity) – of all the positive and negative signs combined: that is, not just human rights, but crimes, catastrophes and accidents which are, it seems, all joyously increasing in the ex-USSR since the liberalization of the regime. And even the rediscovery of pornography and extra-terrestrials, all previously censored, but celebrating their reappearance along with everything else. This is the experimental dimension of this general thaw: we can now see that crimes and catastrophes, both nuclear and natural, along with everything else that has been repressed, are all part of our human rights (the religious sphere too, of course, and fashion; indeed, nothing is debarred) – and this is a fine object lesson in democracy. For we see re-emerging here all that we are, all the allegedly universal emblems of the human in a kind of ideal hallucination and return of the repressed, including the worst, corniest, most banal things in Western 'culture' – things which will henceforth know no boundaries. It is, then, a moment of truth for that culture, as was the earlier confrontation

* For the background to the 'memory of water' affair, see Philippe Alfonsi, *Au nom de la science.*

with the primitive cultures of the whole world, from which our culture cannot really be said to have emerged with flying colours. The irony of the situation is such that it will perhaps be we who are one day forced to rescue the historical memory of Stalinism, while the countries of Eastern Europe will no longer remember the phenomenon. It will be up to us to keep on ice the memory of this tyrant who, for his part, kept the movement of history frozen, since that glacial age also forms part of our universal heritage.

These events are remarkable from another point of view too. They force us to enquire into the turn history is now taking; not proceeding towards its end (a notion that was part of the fantasy of a linear history), but moving into reverse and into systematic obliteration. We are in the process of wiping out the entire twentieth century, effacing all the signs of the Cold War one by one, perhaps even all trace of the Second World War and of all the political or ideological revolutions of the twentieth century. The reunification of Germany is inevitable, as are many other things, not in the sense that they represent a leap forward in history, but as a topsy-turvy rewriting of the whole of the twentieth century, a rewriting which is going to take up a large part of the last ten years of the century. At the rate we are going we shall soon be back at the Holy Roman Empire. And perhaps this is the illumination this *fin de siècle* offers and the true meaning of that controversial formula 'the end of history'. The fact is that, in a sort of enthusiastic work of mourning, we are in the process of retracting all the significant events of this century, of *whitewashing* it, as if everything that had taken place (revolutions, the division of the world, exterminations, the violent transnationality of states, nuclear cliffhanging) – in short, history in its modern phase – were merely a hopeless imbroglio, and everyone had set about undoing that history with the same enthusiasm that had gone into making it. Restoration, regression, rehabilitation, revival of the old frontiers, of the old differences, of particularities, of religions – and even resipiscence in the sphere of morals. It seems that all the signs of liberation achieved over a century are fading and will in the end perhaps be snuffed out one by one: we are engaged in a gigantic process of *revisionism* – not an ideological revisionism but a revisionism of history itself, and we seem in a hurry to finish it before the end of the century, secretly hoping perhaps to be able to start again from scratch in the new millennium. If only we could restore everything to its initial state. But which initial state? Before the twentieth century? Before the Revolution? How far can this reabsorption, this retraction take us? The fact is that it can move very, very quickly (as the events in Eastern Europe show), precisely because it is not a work of construction but a massive deconstruction of history, and one assuming almost a viral, epidemic form.

The strategy of dissolution

All forms of repentance are tiresome, as are all commemorations, since they merely serve as illustrations of repentance. In this sense, even the events in Eastern Europe, even the fantastic *aggiornamento* of the satellite states and the USSR, though that has nothing of the commemoration about it, are also illustrations of this repentance of history, this movement of *istoria repentita*. Neither a regression, nor an end, but a repentance.

The figure of the *pentito* appeared in Italy at the turn of the 1980s. It emerged from within the ultra-left, at the farthest outpost of political modernity, and, in a way, marks that movement's post-modern turn. The *pentiti* suddenly went back on all their previous beliefs and thus came to serve liberal society as a vaccine against all radical temptations. A conversion of this kind was previously unthinkable (the Moscow trials are still about self-criticism, which is a modern value, whereas repentance is post-modern). But this is merely a first phase of a general reversion which does not stop at the extremes: repentance passed first from ultra-leftism to communism, then to the whole of the revolutionary movement. It affected the avant-gardes first, the cutting edge of modernity, then washed back into the central mass, into collective ideologies. The whole of history is repenting the 'excesses' of modernity (and Stalinism was certainly one of those excesses). But, above and beyond the excesses, the whole movement of modernity is affected. It is not just the revolution that is approaching the moment of repentance, but the evolutionary movement of modernity itself.

Repentance is part of post-modernity – the recycling of past forms, the exalting of residues, rehabilitation by *bricolage*, eclectic sentimentality. With a tendency towards high dilution and low intensities. In this sense, Stalinism was modernity and recent events of 'liberation' would represent, rather, a postmodern drop in voltage. And, indeed, the astonishing ease with which they have occurred, their rapidity, is an obvious sign that we are tumbling down the slope of history. Instead of seeing these events as representing more modernity, history or liberty, one might ask if this is not an entropic process. Does this recouping of the democratic deficit, this alignment with a model of easy-going, laid-back freedom, this dislocation of a bloc of otherness represent an increase in energy and complexity or the dissipation of potential energy, energy leaking away as heat? Admittedly, the world gets warmer this way, but does it not thereby reach a more advanced stage of superficial energy – that of communication, of mere heat exchange – the lowest form of energy? The rule today is that everything must go into global circulation. Every event which has its place in the round of liberation is merely the extension of a physical model of circulation and communication, of a dominant model of consensus and regulation of exchanges, and in this sense profoundly wearisome (the form it takes may, however, be original and have extraordinary consequences – May '68, for example, was a politically lightweight episode, but the event was an inspired one).

Moreover, what are the countries of Eastern Europe to be opened up to now that they have been liberated? To the liberal configuration of human rights and a market economy. But the liberal economy which is triumphant today is by no means the initial, historic, modern version of the market economy. We are in an expurgated version, purged of all its contradictions, of the conflictual infrastructure which was that of historic (one might say heroic) capitalism. It is a market economy with no social force to battle against it, no competitive force to drive it on, no collective project to propel it into the future. In short, an economy which is no longer political but transpolitical, and perhaps even transeconomic in its incoherence – an economy of speculation and virtual collapse. Production, the market, ideology, profit and utopia (profit itself is a utopia) were all modern. The competitive capitalist economy was modern. Ours, unreal and speculative, lacking even the notion of production, profit and progress, is no longer modern, but post-modern. And if the countries of Eastern Europe gain access to that economy, they will be entering not the modern but the post-modern era.

The same goes for the 'liberal economy' of human rights. Entire peoples are rushing towards a 'historical' objective of liberty which no longer exists at all in the form in which they imagine it, towards a form of 'democratic' representation which has also long been dying from speculation (the statistical speculation of opinion polls, the media speculation of news [*l'information*]). The democratic illusion is universal, linked as it is to the zero degree of civic energy. All we have left of liberty is an ad-man's illusion, that it, the zero degree of the Idea, and it is this which sets the tone for our liberal regime of human rights.

We all dream, no doubt, in some collective unconscious, of the resurrection of history, but we should not take our dreams for realities. This confused state of thawing relations, of rehabilitation, of liberal redemption and support for human rights is part of a reheating of history, not a revolutionary ferment. Ecstasy and beatification should not be confused. We are currently right in the middle of a phase of beatification, of religious consensus on established (or already lost) values. Which explains, by the way, the astonishing pre-eminence in the media of the figure of the Pope, who travels the whole world (even the Islamic Sahel!) blessing all forms of crossbreeding and repentance, while ensuring that durable forms of voluntary servitude are in place. Formal religion is extending its grasp, just as the speculative economy is extending its own through the Stock Exchange and capital movements. In the new forms of religion, as in the new forms of speculation, we are witnessing the striking illustration of what Hegel calls 'the life, moving within itself, of that which is dead'.*

Something else provides a hint that what is happening in Eastern Europe is not a real historical leap forward – the strange ease with which all the communist regimes collapsed. They were not defeated: they had only to be touched for them to realize that they no longer existed. It was like a cartoon, where the tightrope-walker, teetering over the abyss, suddenly sees his rope is gone and immediately falls, passing without transition from the imaginary to the real (this is the basic mechanism of cartoons). The magical collapse of meaning in the verbal joke is of the same order. In the *Witz*, it is as though the linear structure of language had never existed and suddenly collapses of its own accord with incomprehensible obviousness. What is involved here is not a 'liberation' of language, nor its dislocation as an effect of unconscious contents, but an extreme, accidental form in which language seems to wish to go beyond its intentional operation and get caught up in its own dizzy whirl. Freud saw very well those strange attractors that are condensation, displacement, ellipsis and reversibility. Forms, not values. And recent events have to be seen in terms of a theory of forms, rather than any kind of theory based on relations of force. The communist systems did not succumb to an external enemy, nor even to an internal one (had that been the case, they would have resisted), but to their own inertia, taking advantage of the opportunity, as it were, to disappear (perhaps they were weary of existing). Entire systems lost their immunity and collapsed into themselves, like those buildings subtly dynamited in advance. They sank into their own void. Now, this form of progression, of chain reaction, of superconductivity of events is a marvellous one, like the form of the joke, like all that eludes the rational laws of communication. What took place in Eastern Europe did not come about through ideology and historical violence. It was an almost viral event, and thus mysterious in its form – rather like everything that comes to

* 'Das sich in sich selbst bewegende Leben des Totes'.

us today through the channel of models and images. This is now the only impressive form and can itself act as a strange attractor – on the West in particular.

The spectacle of those regimes imploding with such ease ought to make Western governments – or what is left of them – tremble, for they have barely any more existence than the Eastern ones. In 1968, we saw government authority collapse almost without violence, as if convinced of its non-existence by the mere mirror of the crowds and the street. And the images which came to us from Prague and Berlin were '68-style images, with the same atmosphere, the same faces. The non-existence of governmental power is, admittedly, less visible in the West, on account of its great dilution and the transparency which enables it to survive. In the East, it was opaque and highly concentrated, to the point that, as with an unstable crystal, only an extra little dose was needed for it to liquefy.

It is possible, then, that the countries of Eastern Europe will pass on to us this model of viral collapse, of a virulence deconstructive of power. In exchange, we might pass on to them our liberal virus, our compulsion for objects and images, media and communication, a virus, in our case, which devastates civil society. One virus for another. At bottom, this could be seen as the last episode in the Cold War, a kind of reciprocal contamination between the two blocs formerly shielded from one another by the existence of the Wall. Behind the apparent victory of the West, it is clear, on the contrary, that the strategic initiative came from the East, not by aggression this time, but by disintegration, by a kind of offensive self-liquidation, catching the whole of the West unawares. In the eternal state of deterrence between the two blocs, a situation from which there was no apparent issue, the advantage could be gained only by the side which, one way or another, ended up disarmed. By force of circumstance, which may have equated with a perception of his own weakness, Gorbachev was able to take this strategic tack of disarmament, the real deconstruction of his own bloc, and thereby of the entire world order. This was, in a way, dying communism's witty parting shot, since the quasi-voluntary destabilization of the Eastern bloc, with the complicity of its peoples, is also a destabilization of the West.

Let us beware of the naïve vision of a frozen history suddenly awakening and automatically heading once again, like a turtle, for the sea (for democracy). Things are much more complicated than that.

Now that the problem of the Wall is out of the way, we can see that it perhaps provided more protection for the West than for Eastern Europe. Now that the triumphal illusion of the West annexing the East – for the greater glory of democracy, of course – has faded, we can sense that it might be the other way about: the East gobbling up the West by blackmailing it with poverty and human rights.

The East's great weapon is no longer the H-bomb, but Chernobyl. It is the accident, the accidental virus, the virus of its own decomposition – Chernobyl whose radioactive cloud, by crossing frontiers with far greater ease than armoured divisions, prefigured the collapse of the Wall and the progressive con-tamination of the Western world. Bush may well disarm in the pretence of having won the Cold War, but it is the USSR and Gorbachev who invented the real *bombe à dépression*, the surest one, the one which turns its own depression into a bomb.*

The Eastern bloc cheerfully destroying its own ideological and bureaucratic foundations is more than a twist or ruse of history; it is a joke, a witty stroke of ironic inversion which forces us to read history the other way around. Perhaps such an involuntary challenge could only come from within the confines of an empire which had shown no glimmer of irony, except the crepuscular variety, for half a century. German would describe this kind of transcendent high spirits, of historical rejoicing in sudden change, as *Übermut*. True freedom is certainly not that of human rights, but the freedom which springs from this ironic turn taken by history (current events are never outdone for irony, even in the West: to see Noriega flouting Bush and taking refuge in the Vatican chancellery is not without its comic side).

However this may be, what is going to come of this transfusion

---

* 'Une bombe à dépression' is a fuel-air explosive device, such as the CBU 55-Bs which were used by the Americans to 'clear' jungle areas in Vietnam.

of Good and Evil, beyond the dusting off of liberties and the realignment of democratic façades, remains a mystery.

For Evil is not simply the repressed. If it were only that, it would be sufficient merely to lift the repression weighing upon it, to 'liberate' it, as is being done everywhere (in particular in the East where the barrier of Evil has been broken down). But we are soon going to see that Evil is something different, that it easily outlasts all liberation and that, in dismantling the visible Evil empire, the deeper form of maleficence is simultaneously being liberated. Evil takes advantage of transparency (glasnost) and becomes the transparence of things themselves.

Evil was visible, opaque, localized in the territories of the East. We have exorcized it, liberated it, liquidated it. But has it, for all that, ceased to be Evil? Not at all: it has become fluid, liquid, interstitial, viral. That is the transparence of Evil. It is not that it is transparent [*est transparent*] in the sense that you might see through it. It is, rather, that it shows though [*transparaît*] in all things when they lose their image, their mirror, their reflection, their shadow, when they no longer offer any substance, distance or resistance, when they become both immanent and elusive from an excess of fluidity and luminosity. So long as Evil was opaque, obscene, oblique, obscure, there was still a transcendence of Evil and it could be held at a distance. It has now become immanent and interstitial (in the West, it is assuming, in particular, the form of terrorism as a filterable virus. Political terrorism, but also all the other forms of virulence – biological, sexual, media-based or electronic). With the events in Eastern Europe, this theme is given striking illustration, and Evil is entering upon a phase of definitive dissemination. Shattered, destabilized communism will pass into the veins of the West in metabolic, surreptitious form, and destabilize it in its turn. This will no longer be the violence of the Idea, but the virus of de-immunization. A communism which dissolves itself is a successful communism.

One of the consequences of this East–West transfusion is the elimination of the renegades who functioned as an umbilical cord between the two blocs, condemned on the one side, fêted on the other, but complicit with both. By way of dissidents – the political avant-garde of the Eastern bloc countries and refuge of the Western intellectual avant-garde – East and West carried on a kind of dialogue of the deaf throughout all the years of the arms race. Some among the dissidents have analysed the ambiguity of this situation. Including Sakharov himself. But Sakharov is dead. He died, significantly, when dissidence, victorious, no longer had any meaning. Dissidents cannot bear a thaw. They have to die, or else become president (Walesa, Havel) in a sort of bitter revenge which, at any event, marks their death as dissidents. They lived in the silent cinema of the political; the 'talkie' era kills them off. They whose strength was in silence (or censorship) are condemned to speak and be devoured by speech. When the Eastern bloc societies catch up with their dissidents and absorb them, it is the end of modernity, as it is when Western society catches up with and absorbs its avant-gardes. In the East and the West, the Idea is finished. The organic consensus marks the dawning of post-modern societies, non-conflictual and at one with themselves. The collapse of the Wall is the visible outward manifestation of an invisible event which has affected all these societies for at least twenty years: the collapse of the division or split internal to each of them, of the conflictual structure which came about with the upheavals and revolutions of the modern era.

The Western intellectuals who embodied that split, that internal division of societies and minds, are themselves fated to disappear like the silent movie actors.

As for those who were pro-dissident in the West, the fine-spirited sympathizers, what is to become of their solidarity? They too are condemned. They spoke for others. Will they now have the courage to shut up? They will not, and are already running off to the scene of the crime, to the Berlin Wall, for that was indeed the site of the crime and the sacrifice. The point when the Wall comes down marks the end of their careers. There is no longer any abominable Other (the communists), no longer any adorable Other (the dissidents).

What of Zinoviev? What of his cynical, merrily nihilistic and paradoxical line (Cioran: history is dying for want of paradoxes)?

The paradox of communism, in Zinoviev's view, is that of being at one and the same time an outdated solution, an end of history, the Evil empire *and* the definitive solution because it has experienced the worst, as the West has not done, and has drawn the consequences from it. It is therefore a solution from after the catastrophe (whatever it may be, whether Third World War or something else), a final solution to the survival of the species and thus an inevitable and definitive model, while nonetheless one that is outdated at the level of the economy and history. This paradox is going to become highly charged when put to the test by the reunification of the two worlds. For the human and ideological failure of communism by no means compromises its potency and virulence as an anthropological model. It is a kind of gigantic snare of the social and the political spheres, which might be said to have succeeded, even if it destroys itself — particularly if it destroys itself — in a kind of *stratégie du pire* which would be imposed on everyone as the last immune defence, *man being taken in hand*, on a universal scale, *to protect him from himself*. On the opposite side, there is only the transparency of democracy, incapable of containing the radiation of Evil.

There is, moreover, a paradox of Western societies opposite and equivalent to that of communism: though they present all the signs of more developed and open societies, at the same time they have one eye on the past as though it were a void they have created behind them, while absorbing the future. It is like the story of the lorry and the hole: some workers dig a hole and load it on to a lorry, but when they hit a bump in the road the hole falls off and, reversing, the lorry falls into the hole. We are the lorry and the hole: we are weighed down by a hole in our memories, weighed down by the retrospective emptiness of our history, to the point that our societies do not even know whether they are heading towards the future. They are riding the surf of their present, problematic wealth. Beneath their apparent mobility and acceleration, they have come to a stop in their hearts and their aims. That is, indeed, why they are accelerating, but they are doing so out of inertia.

The encounter between this type of society with maximum

mobility but immobility in its heart and the Eastern bloc societies which are petrified on the outside but in no way inert in their inward core should be highly dramatic or totally ambiguous. Like blood transfusions today, the transfusion of Good and Evil presents many dangers. There is a risk we shall pass all our germs on to them, and they might give us all of theirs (this is how contacts between dissimilar cultures or races go). First of all, there will be seventy years of 'backwardness' to make up, but are we so sure things are going to happen that way? Instead of the Eastern bloc countries accelerating towards modern democracy, perhaps we are going to drift in the other direction, moving back beyond democracy and falling into the hole of the past. It would be the opposite of Orwell's prediction (strangely, he has not been mentioned of late, though the collapse of Big Brother ought to have been celebrated for the record, if only for the irony of the date Orwell set for the onset of totalitarianism which turned out to be roughly that of its collapse). Even more ironic is the fact that we are not at all threatened by the totalitarian (Stalinist) rewriting of the past, but the democratic rewriting of history: the very images of Stalin and Lenin swept away, streets and cities renamed, statues scattered, soon none of all that will have existed. Yet another ruse of history – not the last but, as ever, the best.

Democratic rewriting. The scenario is off to a good start. Everyone is having a clear-out. All the dictatorships are being wound up and sold off cheap, before the end of the century if possible (before Christmas for Eastern Europe so that everything can shine bright in a new Nativity). Splendid emulation, as stupendous as the tolerance which has reigned over it all so far. Everyone equally committed to the liquidation! Eliminating the planet's blackspots as one might eliminate traffic accident blackspots, as we might eliminate spots from a face: cosmetic surgery elevated to the level of the political, and to Olympic performance levels.

Of course, this great democratic rally is not believable for an instant. Not that there is any Machiavellian strategy going on, but it's too good to be true. There is something suspect about the sudden consensus. The disappearance, as if by magic, of all contradiction is more than suspect (China has temporarily relapsed, and what remains of world communism is merely a theme park. With a little imagination, Cuba could be joined up with Disneyworld, which is not far away, as part of a world heritage centre). Something tells us that what we have here is not a historical evolution, but an *epidemic* of consensus, an epidemic of democratic values – in other words, this is a viral effect, a triumphant effect of fashion. If democratic values spread so easily, by a capillary or communicating-vessels effect, then they must have liquefied, they must now be worthless. Throughout the modern age they were held dear and dearly bought. Today, they are being sold off at a discount and we are watching a Dutch auction of democratic values which looks very much like uncontrolled speculation. Which makes it highly probable that, as might be the case with financial speculation, these same values may crash.

It is clear that the ultimate deterrence has come from the East – no longer that of the balance of terror, which, for forty years, prevented the event of atomic war from coming about, but of the imbalance of terror, which prevents the confrontation itself from coming about. Deterrence by self-dissolution, demolition, de-escalation, unilateral disarmament, auto-destabilization which completely destabilizes the opponent – a strategy of weakness, an unexpected, unpredictable strategy even for the protagonists themselves, but all the more effective for that. A strategy of dis-appearance, dispersion, dissemination, contamination, virulence by fragmentation. For not only are the weapons, hardware and brains of the former USSR going to turn up all over the world, but the model of disintegration is going to radiate out also, more effective than a thousand atom bombs. Integral, totalitarian communism could be sealed up and neutralized. Disintegrated communism becomes viral; it becomes capable of passing through its own wall and infecting the whole world, not by ideology or by its model of functioning, but by its model of dysfunctioning and of sudden, violent destructuring. Certainly, we might ask whether this is still communism? Whatever the answer, it is exerting an influence over the world which it could never muster by arms or by thought, an influence over the whole world by the event of its disappearance. In that sense, it might be said that it is triumphant, since perfect communism, the fully realized communism, like the fully realized utopia, is the one which has disappeared. In that sense, too, the consequences of communism's sudden self-dissolution are perhaps even more incalculable than those of its appearance at the dawn of this century. Not through ideology, but through the *auto-da-fé* of its own principles, the unconditional acting out of capitulation. In terms of ideas, it had opened up a monolithic, totalitarian path; with its inverted acting out, it opens up the path of dislocation for all structures and empires. The East will have victoriously countered capital with capitulation.

It is Chernobyl that will turn out to have been the real starting point in this involuntary, but brilliant strategic inversion which has destabilized the very concept of relations of force, creating out of this a strategy of relations of weakness and completely changing the rules of the game. Up to that point, things were frozen: no military, offensive acting-out was possible. Everything culminated in Star Wars, an impossible scenario: orbital bombs are virtual; they do not explode. The only true bomb explodes – or implodes – on the spot, by superfusion: Chernobyl, an accidental acting-out. It was the Eastern bloc that exploded that bomb in its own heart and it was that bomb which, in the form of the first atomic cloud, crossed the Wall and frontiers without encountering any opposition, inaugurating the fusion between the two worlds by radioactive infiltration. So the initial explosion of the New World Order will indeed have come from the East, and the contamination has passed from East to West. After Chernobyl, the Berlin Wall no longer exists. Symbolically, it is therefore nuclear fusion, after all, which presides over the political, transpolitical confusion of the blocs. By the suicidal accident of Chernobyl, the former USSR both admits its impotence, its weakness, and at the same time passes the whole lot over to the

West, obliging it to manage the collapse, to manage a whole world gone bankrupt. That of communism to begin with, but soon, subtly, the world of capital itself. Up to now, communism had sought out the weakest link in the capitalist chain. Suddenly, it discovered that *it* was the weakest link and, by destroying itself, by cracking up almost accidentally, it sent the other world hurtling to its doom, forced it to deny itself as enemy, contaminated its defences, exported its own economic and political suicide. The captive hell of communism found itself liberated. From this point on, the barrier separating hell from heaven is liquidated. And in this case, of course, the liquefaction is general, and hell always submerges heaven.

Solzhenitsyn writes (against Sakharov and his idea of having the two hostile blocs converge so as to unite their mutual qualities): 'What can come of two societies afflicted with such redhibitory vices when they come closer together and are transformed by the contact between them? A society twice as immoral.' The dream of plurality is indeed precisely this: differences are to be exchanged as positive qualities. Whereas what always wins out in the exchange of differences, in dialogue, is the exchange and addition of negative qualities. Fusion always turns into confusion, contact into contamination. We have an example of this today with AIDS and the fatal potentiality threatening every sexual encounter. But the same goes for computers: maximum interconnectedness brings maximum vulnerability of all networks (the trend now is towards stand-alone computers; it seems in fact that networks transmit viruses even faster than information). Genetic confusion runs in this same direction. It is one of the aspects of the principle of Evil that it always proceeds more quickly than Good.

So Solzhenitsyn, for his part objecting to this immoral confusion, is right and Sakharov wrong. But we have nothing against vice and immorality. If they have to be increased in the confusion of the two worlds, then perhaps that is better, all in all, than the austere, puritanical order of deterrence and the balance of terror. Why not a world society which is entirely corrupt, a single empire which is the empire of confusion, a New World

Disorder which combines the filterable viruses of communism with the discreet charm of the rights of man and nature?

It might seem that the flow of wealth and abundance moving from West to East wins out over the opposite flow. But what flows from West to East is chiefly the illusion of victory. What is moving in the other direction is more subtle and more deadly: the virus of weakness, the multiple forms of disaffection, the end of all democratic illusions. In short, nothing is decided and no one can say who will win, who will be first to destabilize the other, the rich, business-like countries or those trained by Marxism in abulia and corruption? Slackness or efficiency? Fatal apathy or high performance levels? The captive hell of paradise or the captive paradise of hell? The two worlds now stand opposed not with weapons or ideas, but mentally in the artificial promiscuity of the New World Order. This is where the transparence of Evil begins. This is where we shall see, once all the conditions for order are fulfilled, how irresistible is disorder; once all the conditions for Good are fulfilled, how irresistible is Evil, how it circulates in the same arterial system as Good and feeds off it, in all innocence, in all perversity. It is Dracula against Snow White (the Dracula myth is gathering strength all around as the Faustian and Promethean myths fade). We have a good idea who is going to suck the other's blood once their glass coffins are broken open.

It is in Germany that these two worlds are telescoped together, with Berlin as the epicentre, since there, paradoxically, it is from reunification that the antagonism arises. It is not the confrontation but the rapprochement of two worlds which produces violence and the clash of mentalities. The historical failure of the one, when faced with the dazzling success of the other, may turn to defiance, and those very people who eyed the wealth enviously when it was still forbidden may very well turn their backs entirely on the Western model merely to remain consistent with themselves. In the course of their misfortunes, the people of Eastern Europe have certainly acquired an opinion on history and its perverse effects. Against all theoretical predictions, out of the two opposed worlds of Capital and Labour, it is that of Labour they have seen collapse. Logically, they must have drawn from this a lesson of non-labour and collective irresponsibility. However this may be, it will certainly not be easy to convert them to the liberal cult of performance.

This is how the reversal of Western values begins. Not merely by the infiltration into the metropolitan heartland of a Fourth World which, unlike the Third, has no other territory than the one it destabilizes from within, but also by the osmosis of an Eastern European world which is decomposing, and making of that decomposition if not a strategy then at least a trap, a decoy, a *politique du pire*. Now, we know that one of the characteristics of the West, represented to perfection by the Americans in the recent Gulf War, is a tendency to shoot at decoys.

The drip-feeding of Western values behind the Iron Curtain gives way today to the percolation, the surreptitious infiltration of the impotence, slackness, technological, economic and demographic ill-will of another world that was long considered residual, backward, under-developed and which is rising up today as a fully fledged protagonist, an equal protagonist and perhaps even a superior one to the extent that *its potential of impotence is superior to our potential of potency*. Now, contrary to the apparent facts which suggest that all cultures are penetrable by the West – that is, corruptible by the universal – it is the West which is eminently penetrable. The other cultures (including those of Eastern Europe), even when they give the impression of selling themselves, of prostituting themselves to material goods or Western ideologies, in fact remain impenetrable behind the mask of prostitution. They can be wiped out physically and morally, but not penetrated. This alienness is linked to their complicity with themselves. The West, for its part, is alien to itself, and anyone can just walk right in.

The logic of this challenge is alien to that of the economic and liberal New World Order. In the order of power and wealth, one desires the death of the other so as to take his place. By contrast, what these refractory, incompatible cultures want, what they demand, is not to take the place but to see the death of the West, even at the risk of dying themselves. The West, naïve as ever, believes it is resented for its power and wealth and, even more naïvely, believes in the compatibility of all cultures. But even when the 'others' seem to be demanding their share of the cake, this is still an allegorical way of desiring its death.

The West is discovering the Eastern bloc countries, weak and drained, as once it discovered the survivors of the concentration camps. The danger is to feed them too quickly, since this kills them. But, in any case, whether or not they are saved, they live in another space – shattered by catastrophe. They will never come back into ours. Certainly, we shall do all we can to wipe this past from their memories. But in vain. It is they, by contrast, who will suck us into their empty space, just as the dead and the survivors of the camps have sucked our last vague desires for culture, law and morality into the empty space and impotent memory of extermination. The attraction of the void is irresistible. The 'victory' of the West is not unlike a depressurizing of the West in the void of communism, in the void of history.

All that began with Chernobyl, as a cold, almost involuntary, strategy, is still going its merry way. Ten or twenty Soviet nuclear power stations sit there, awaiting fissure and meltdown, like a time-bomb that cannot be defused, prolonging the suspense of a phoney, cold war, which, being accidental, would offer no possibility of retaliation. On the contrary, indeed, the enemy is forced to take you in hand to avoid catastrophe. The whole strategy of the ex-Empire is organized in this way – at great cost in poverty, radiation or civil war – around the black hole into which it might itself be said to have fallen, but into which it is dragging all its old adversaries, one after another, along with history itself, causing this latter to ebb back to an uncertain past, a foetal stage where the phantoms of the old conflicts and the old nationalisms bump up against the ghost of the atomic weapons which are now rendered useless (and which it will hence be possible to spread around generously).

To this, we must add the dispersal by auction of the Soviet army which, like the state, is being sold off for spares. We had never seen anything like this before – the strongest state and largest army in the world fainting right away. We have not taken this great world premiere fully on board. Let us hope it is merely a dress rehearsal. What should have been a source of universal rejoicing passed off almost without interest – a sign of the nullity of the age. But we have to understand what this break-up of the Red Army and the selling-off of its nuclear forces will mean. It amounts to their dispersal over the whole of the globe. Once the reference point of its intended usage is gone, weaponry, like the atom, becomes viral and interstitial.

The illusion is, in fact, to believe that the collapse of the great empires opens up a renewal of history, whereas it merely opens out on to the metastases of empire. The most probable hypothesis is that we are dealing here not with a disappearance, but with a dispersal of empire into all the local, provincial, territorial micro-empires. This is the same homology between the detail and the whole as in holograms: the mirror of the empire is broken, but each fragment preserves its image. The great dismantled systems (and the process isn't over yet; just wait for the end of the American Empire and the 'historic' nations) find the means to perpetuate themselves in another way, not by dynastic filiation as in the past, but by something like fractal division, by scissiparity: micro-imperia, micro-dictatorships, micro-autarkies bearing within themselves, in miniature, all the stigmata and vices of empire. Reintroducing the same servitude, this time administered at the level of identity (whether the identity of the individual, the group, the ethnic group or the enterprise). The end of empires means the unrestricted reign of slave micro-systems. Even in the end of the nuclear empire we find this same trend: the dispersal of atomic weapons will have the effect of enslaving the other nations to the same system of deterrence, the same consensual equilibrium.

And what of the political in all this? That died with the great empires. Their perpetuation in other forms – fragmented, irradiated, decentred, peripheral – the second life of the great empires in retroviral form, so to speak, genetically infecting all their wastes, all their by-products, all their basic cells, is no longer of the order of the political, but of the transpolitical. A flabby, decentred, high-dilution transpolitical, where ideological options are immaterial and historical violence minimal (in most conflicts, the violence is merely a homeopathic, police violence, internal to the systems).

To all intents and purposes, the political died with the historical passions aroused by the great ideas and the great empires. The transpolitical, for its part, has but a single passion: that of the work of mourning and recycling (intellectuals are passing through the same phase: the work of mourning for morality and the universal conscience). And a single, inexhaustible energy – for managing residues. The new labour power, which has emerged in this *fin de siècle*, is mourning power. The energy of the corpse is recycled, just as Romain Gary recycled the spiritual charge of dead souls as material energy ('the charge of souls'), and as Jarry had dead men pedalling – henceforth indefatigable since they were pedalling by inertia. As something which has failed, this work of mourning is interminable; it becomes lost in the melancholy of homeopathic and homeostatic systems, where even the recognition of death, the intuition of that death (of the political), is impossible, since it would reintroduce a fatal virus into the virtual immortality of the transpolitical. There is the same problem with freedom: the least reinjection of a dose of freedom, or even of a problematic of freedom, would introduce a fatal virus into the chain of networks, the virus of voluntary servitude – a non-violent, consensual, ecological micro-servitude, which is everywhere the successor to totalitarian oppression.

The most amusing feature of this history, the ironic thing about the end, is that communism should have collapsed exactly as Marx had foreseen for capitalism, with the same suddenness, and, ultimately, with such ease that it did not even strike the imagination. The fact that he got the victor wrong in no way detracts from the exactness of Marx's analysis; it merely adds the objective irony which was lacking. Fate took care of that. It is as though some evil genie had substituted the one for the other – communism for capitalism – at the last moment. As if, since

Western society had, in its own way, brought to fruition the prophecies of a future society (the withering away of the State, of the political, of work, the administration of things and generalized leisure — even if all these are simulated) in communism's stead, the latter could simply disappear. An admirable division of labour: Capital has done communism's work and communism has died in Capital's place. But this can just as easily turn around. For all these ideal perspectives, including that of theoretical communism, were perhaps merely absurd. Capital, for its part, ended up achieving the objective of *real* communism, which was generalized exchange. At any price. Precisely at any price, indeed, since it achieved it under the auspices of the market and the commodity. But this too is part of the irony of history: the inversion of the final meaning — the final illusion. One cannot ask events to be true to the initial conditions. They sometimes occur in exactly the opposite way, in an ironic mode, while engendering the same final conditions.

Capital has cannibalized all negativity, that of history and that of work in a — literally — sarcastic fashion: devouring the very substance of the human being to transform it into its essence as productive being. It has unceremoniously devoured the dialectic by parodistically taking the opposing terms upon itself, by parodistically going beyond its own contradictions. What we see before us is the parodic triumph of the classless society, the parodic realization of all utopian metaphors: the man of leisure, transdisciplinary pluralism, the mobility and availability of all signs — the cook become head of state, or almost (we have seen worse since this old dream of Lenin's). Unfortunately, in the meantime, the State has disappeared, or almost disappeared, doubtless as a result of the same effect which enables the cook to accede to its head, without it being possible to say whether the disappearance of the one brought about the promotion of the other, or the other way about. But, in any case, when the State ceases to be the State, the cook ceases to be the cook. As Brecht says, the fact that beer is not beer is harmoniously compensated by the fact that the cigar is not a cigar either. Thus the ironic order is safe and sound.

The other irony of history is the Ubuesque form of repentance. Gorbachev is giving up Marxism! Fantastic! But what does 'giving up' mean? Can you give up Marxism in the way you give up tobacco or alcohol? Can you give up your father and mother? Can you give up God? In its time, the Church has come close to giving up the Devil or the Immaculate Conception, but this has not occurred. Renunciation is the symmetrical and opposite movement to faith – as absurd and useless. If things exist, there is no use believing in them. If they do not exist, there is no use renouncing them. So the renunciation of the class struggle is grotesque: you can deny the class struggle or sacrifice it if you have to, but you can't give it up like an old skin or a childhood superstition.

This renunciation, this apostasy, is a very bad example. What if one day the West too were to renounce capitalism. And what if, one day, the West were forced to revive Marxism, which is, after all, part of our heritage, damn it (as also is damnation).*

---

* 'Et si un jour l'Occident était forcé de ressusciter le marxisme, qui fait quand même partie du patrimoine, que diable (le Diable aussi d'ailleurs).' I have departed slightly from the French text here in order to retain the pun.

The Timişoara massacre

Yet it seems we are tired of fuelling the end of history with simulacra and are now letting it follow out its course; we are tired of that long simulation of modernity and are entering, with recent events – including those in Eastern Europe – upon a phase of *desimulation*. The Gulf War and the events in Eastern Europe are among those quasi-unreal events which have less meaning in themselves than in the fact that they put an end to things which long ago ceased to have meaning (communism in the Eastern bloc countries, the Cold War for the Gulf). In this sense, they are, after all, symptomatic, but ambiguous events – immediately credible (via the media), but fundamentally undecidable. Retrospectively, it is the same with many past or recent events: they too are not of the order of truth, but of credibility. News [*information*] makes everything credible (that is, uncertain), even previous facts, even future events. The criteria of truth have been supplanted by the principle of credibility (which is also the principle of statistics and opinion polls), and this is the true guiding principle of news. The uncertainty I am speaking of is like a virus which affects or infects all history, current events and images. Even if it is refuted, it can only be refuted virtually, since virtuality forms part of reality itself – a reality which is now uncertain, paradoxical, random, hyper-real, filtered by the medium, cut adrift by its own image.

Hence the interest of submitting the Gulf War and the

Romanian 'revolution' to this uncertainty test, of adding them to that set of objects which are unverifiable other than on the screens, which immediately degrade into news and are rapidly laundered and forgotten like any other spectacle.

In the case of the Romanian revolution, it was the faking of the dead in Timişoara which aroused a kind of moral indignation and raised the problem of the scandal of 'disinformation' or, rather, of *information itself as scandal*.

It was not the dead that were the scandal, but the corpses being pressed into appearing before the television cameras, as in the past dead souls were pressed into appearance in the register of deaths. It was their being taken hostage, as it were, and our being held hostage too, as mystified TV viewers. Being blackmailed by violence and death, especially in a noble and revolutionary cause, was felt to be worse than the violence itself, was felt to be a parody of history.

All the media live off the presumption of catastrophe and of the succulent imminence of death. A photo in *Libération*, for example, shows us a convoy of refugees 'which, some time after this shot was taken, *was to be* attacked by the Iraqi army'. Anticipation of effects, morbid simulation, emotional blackmail. It was the same on CNN with the arrival of the Scuds. Nothing is news if it does not pass through that horizon of the virtual, that hysteria of the virtual – not in the psychological sense, but in the sense of a compulsion for what is presented, in all bad faith, as real to be consumed as unreal.

In the past, to show something up as a fake, we said: 'It's just play-acting', 'It's all romance!', 'It's put on for the cameras!'. This time, with Romania and the Gulf War, we were able to say, 'It's just TV!'

Photographic or cinema images still pass through the negative stage (and that of projection), whereas the TV image, the video image, digital and synthetic, are images without a negative, and hence without negativity and without reference. They are *virtual* and the virtual is what puts an end to all negativity, and thus to all reference to the real or to events. At a stroke, the contagion of images, engendering themselves without reference to a real or an imaginary, itself becomes virtually without limits, and this limitless engendering produces *information as catastrophe.*

Is an image which refers only to itself still an image? However this may be, that image raises the problem of its indifference to the world, and thus of our indifference to *it* – which is a political problem. When television becomes the strategic space of the event, it sets itself up as a deadly self-reference, it becomes a bachelor machine.* The real object is wiped out by news – not merely alienated, but abolished. All that remains of it are traces on a monitoring screen.

Many Romanian eyewitness accounts speak of being dispossessed of the event in this way, deprived of the lived experience they have of it by being submerged in the media network, by being placed under house arrest in front of their television screens. Spectators then become *exoterics* of the screen, living their revolution as an exoticism of images, themselves exogenous, touristic spectators of a virtual history. From the moment the studio becomes the strategic centre, and the screen the only site of appearance, everyone wants to be on it at all costs, or else gathers in the street in the glare of the cameras, and these, indeed, actually film one another. The street becomes an extension of the studio, that is, of the *non-site* of the event, of the *virtual* site of the event. The street itself becomes a virtual space. Site of the definitive confusion of masses and medium, of the real-time confusion of act and sign.

There is no will to communicate in all this. The only irresistible drive is to occupy this non-site, *this empty space of representation* which is the screen. Representation (political representation too) is currently a trough of depression – meteorological depression – which the media fill up with their turbulences, with the same consequences as occur when any kind of space is suddenly depressurized. The highest pressure of news corresponds to the lowest pressure of events and reality [*le réel*].

* A reference to Michel Carrouges's *Les machines célibataires* and the works by Duchamp et al. which inspired it.

The same unrealism in the Ceauşescu trial. It is not the judicial procedure itself which is scandalous but the video tape, unacceptable as the only, bloodless trace of a bloody event. In the eyes of the whole world, this will remain an event forever suspect, for the sole reason of its – strangely obscene – scenic abduction. This hidden jury, its voice striking out against the accused, these defendants we are forced to see even though they are virtually dead, these dead prisoners shot a second time to meet the needs of news. One might even wonder whether the actors in this staged event were not deliberately trying to make themselves seem suspect in the eyes of world opinion, as though playing at sabotaging their image. At the same time, the Ceauşescu trial was pulled off perfectly as a video production, betraying a sharp sense of the image-function, the blackmail-function, the deterrence-function. Deep down, the intuitive grasp of these things has grown more sophisticated over there, in the shadow of dictatorship, than it has with us. We have nothing to teach them. For, if the Romanians themselves got high on this media speculation which served them as a revolutionary aphrodisiac, they also dragged all the Western media into the same news demagogy. By manipulating themselves, they caused us spontaneously to swallow their fiction. We bear the same responsibility as they do. Or, rather, there is no responsibility anywhere. The question of responsibility cannot even be raised. It is the evil genius of news which promotes such staging.

When information gets mixed in with its source, then, as with sound waves, you get a feedback effect – an effect of interference and uncertainty. When demand is maximal (and everywhere today the demand for events is maximal), it short-circuits the initial situation and produces an uncontrollable response effect. That is, ultimately, why we do the Romanians an injustice when we accuse them of manipulation and bad faith. No one is responsible. It is all an effect of the infernal cycle of credibility. The actors and the media sensed obscurely that the events in Eastern Europe had to be given credibility, that that revolution had to be lent credibility by an extra dose of dead bodies. And the media themselves had to be lent credibility by the reference to the people. Leading to a vicious circle of credibility, the result of which is the *decredibilizing* of the revolution and the events themselves. The logical sequence of news and history turns back against itself, bringing, in its cyclical movement, a kind of deflation of historical consciousness.

The Americans did just the same in the Gulf War. By the excessive nature of their deployment and stagecraft, by putting their power and news control so extravagantly to the test, they decredibilized both war and news. They were the Ubus of their own power, just as the Romanians were the Ubus of their own impotence. Excess itself engenders the parody which invalidates the facts. And, just as the principle of economics is wrecked by financial speculation, so the principle of politics [*le politique*] and history is wrecked by media speculation.

Contrary to the fiction of universal solidarity surrounding the media and images, events have less and less meaning, less and less reality beyond a near horizon. In the media space, the rate of diffusion is maximal, but the resonance factor is zero. In the past, facts and actions had a real resonance within a limited field, a field of organic proximity. The Europe of the fifteenth or eighteenth centuries communicated in a much livelier, freer way than the interactive, TV Europe of the twentieth century. And that 'natural' horizon opened out on to a possible universe, whereas today the universal promiscuity of images reinforces our exile and immures us in our indifference.

We are convinced that the Eastern European powers collapsed because they had infringed the 'natural and democratic' law of news and information. Everything over there was underexposed to the light of human rights and hence unreal and unnatural. For fifty years, we had regarded all these peoples as mystified victims of dictatorship, whose only way out was to be won over to our marvellous values. As if we were not ourselves hostages to a system every bit as terroristic as theirs, the system of fluidity and transparency, a system just as effective at putting an end to history as the Eastern regimes with their bureaucratic deep-freeze. Today, now that transparency (glasnost!) has been achieved, a transparency which turns out of course to be rigged and loaded down with all the detritus of history, one might almost feel sorry that entire peoples are coming out of their darkness, even if it was violent and tyrannical, to fall prey to the Enlightenment, to go down like flies in the artificial light of our freedom, our unbounded solidarity, our unscrupulous news system. We who so respect the private life of individuals should also respect that of peoples and their right – against all international morality – to escape this modern tribunal of news and information-gathering which is assuming all the features of an inquisition. For only information has sovereign rights, since it controls the right to existence.

It is this whole democratic pharisaism of the West that is thwarted by the Romanians' media cynicism, by their radical use of the medium and radical contempt for the message (of course, they are only used here as an example). Ultimately, whether or not they intended to, they have taught us a useful lesson. By parodying it, they have booby-trapped our finest technological gimmick: the image. By handling it unscrupulously, they have destroyed its mythology. And they have also given us a useful lesson in freedom, not by truly achieving liberty, but by ensnaring us in a fantasy of liberation which is, in fact, geared to our Western demand. By their revolutionary *mise en scène*, they sent us the message we were expecting, here employing the mirror trick of conformism which blinds its victims. And we were blinded.

At the same time, they showed us that freedom extended as far as the open, cynical manipulation of the facts, whereas we, for our part, only go so far as their shamefaced manipulation. We confine ourselves to the moral, conditional forms of liberty whereas they go as far as the unconditional, parodic, paroxystic form of liberation of the image, of liberation by the image. It is not clear why, once it had been 'liberated', the image would not be entitled to lie. No doubt this may even be seen as one of its vital functions, and it is naïve to think it was going to liberate itself to bring about truth – just as naïve as thinking that the Romanians were going to liberate themselves to arrive at a 'true' democracy. The truth is that the liberation of the image inclines it quite naturally to simulation, and that is where it finds its true freedom. Though we may not wish to acknowledge this, we have nonetheless to accept the evidence: the image and, with it, news [*l'information*] is not attached to any principle of truth or reality.

Here, then, is the international consciousness foiled by its own ideal, hoist with its own petard. The Gulf War merely accentuated the disastrous impression of our having been drawn so far into simulation that the question of truth and reality cannot even be posed, of our having been drawn so far into the 'liberation' of the medium and the image that the question of freedom cannot even be posed. But can news and the media really be put on trial now? Absolutely not, for the simple reason that the media themselves hold the key to the judicial enquiry. There can be no contesting their innocence since 'disinformation' is always imputed to an accident of news-gathering [*information*]; the guiding principle itself is never questioned.

And yet there will, nonetheless, have been a kind of verdict in this Romanian affair, and the artificial heaps of corpses will have been of some use, all the same. One might ask whether the Romanians, by the very excessiveness of this staged event and the simulacrum of their revolution, have not served as demystifiers of news and its guiding principle. For, if the media image has put an end to the credibility of the event, the event will, in its turn, have put an end to the credibility of the image. Never again shall we be able to look at a television picture in good faith, and this is the finest collective demystification we have ever known. The finest revenge over this new arrogant power, this power to blackmail by events. Who can say what responsibility attaches to the televisual production of a false massacre (Timişoara), as compared with the perpetrating of a true massacre? This is another kind of crime against humanity, a hijacking of fantasies, affects and the credulity of hundreds of millions of people by means of television – a crime of blackmail and simulation. What penalty is laid down for such a hijacking?

There is no way to rectify this situation and we must have no illusions: there is no perverse effect, nor even anything scandalous in the 'Timişoara syndrome'. It is simply the (immoral) truth of news, the secret purpose [*destination*] of which is to deceive us about the real, but also to *undeceive us about the real*. There is no worse mistake than taking the real for the real and, in that sense, the very excess of media illusion plays a vital disillusioning role. In this way, news could be said to undo its own spell by its effects and the violence of information to be avenged by the repudiation and indifference it engenders.

Just as we should be unreservedly thankful for the existence of politicians, who take on themselves the responsibility for that wearisome function, so we should be grateful to the media for existing and taking on themselves the triumphant illusionism of the world of communications, the whole ambiguity of mass culture, the confusion of ideologies, the stereotypes, the spectacle, the banality – soaking up all these things in their operation. While, at the same time, constituting a permanent test of intelligence, for where better than on television can one learn to question every picture, every word, every commentary? Television inculcates indifference, distance, scepticism and unconditional apathy. Through the world's becoming-image, it anaesthetizes the imagination, provokes a sickened abreaction, together with a surge of adrenalin which induces total disillusionment. Television and the media would render reality [*le réel*] dissuasive, were it not already so. And this represents an absolute advance in the consciousness – or the cynical unconscious – of our age.

The illusion of war

Exchanging war for the signs of war.

America conducted the Gulf War as though it were a nuclear conflict, and thus, ultimately, as a substitute for a Third World War which did not take place. An atomic war without the atom, but analogous in its impact, instantaneousness, non-confrontation and convulsive effect. The first strike is the last. That, at least, is how the nuclear shoot-out was supposed to be, but neither of the two adversaries ever risked it, perhaps because, deep down, they neither of them believed in it. The nuclear shoot-out, the game of deterrence, was a scenario, just made credible by the calculated threat of the balance of terror. When the prospect of an atomic clash disappeared once and for all, when it got lost in space with Star Wars, it had to be tested in simulated form, in a miniature war-game where the possibility of annihilating the enemy could be checked out. But, symptomatically, care was taken not to go that far: Saddam, who will, in the end, have been nothing but that fairground dummy you shoot at from point-blank range, had to be saved. It was just a second-hand scenario.

So this military 'orgy' wasn't an orgy at all. It was an orgy of simulation, the simulation of an orgy. A German word sums all this up very well: *Schwindel*, which means both giddiness and swindle, loss of consciousness and mystification.

The Americans fought the same war in respect of world opinion – via the media, censorship, CNN, etc. – as they fought on the battlefield. They used the same 'fuel air' explosives in the media, where they draw all the oxygen out of public opinion.

The amnesia about it is, in itself, a confirmation of the unreality of this war. Overexposed to the media, underexposed to memory. Built-in obsolescence, as with any consumer article . . . Forgetting is built into the event itself in the profusion of information and details, just as obsolescence is built into the object in the profusion of useless accessories.

If you take one-thousandth of what you see on the TV news to heart, you're done for. But television protects us from this. Its immunizing, prophylactic use protects us from an unbearable responsibility. Its effect and its images self-destruct in the mind. So is this the zero degree of communication? Certainly, it is: people fear communication like the plague.

There was no exulting after the Gulf War either (and yet, it was a victory, wasn't it?). There was, rather, a flight into amnesia and hypocrisy. A botched operation, even in surgical terms: its labours produced nothing, even the two hundred thousand dead produced nothing, apart from that marvellous miscarriage, the New World Order. It was a war without results, but not without an aftermath. Once past the dilemma of the reality/unreality of the war, we are back in the pure and simple reality of political ignominy, in the most odious *Realpolitik*: the Shi'ites, the Kurds, the calculated survival of Saddam . . . Here, the most fervent defenders of the war's reality end up conceding that perhaps nothing has in fact happened. But they prejudge this from the absence of an outcome; they do not judge the event itself. Which shows them to be just as much engaged in *Realpolitik* as anyone else.

The question is not whether one is for or against war, but whether one is for or against *the reality of war*. Analysis must not be sacrificed to the expression of anger. It has to be directed in its entirety against reality, against manifestness – here against the manifest reality of this war. The Stoics contest the very self-evidence of pain, when the body's confusion is at its height. Here, we must contest the very self-evidence of war, when the confusion of the real is at its height. We must hit out at the weak point of reality. It's too late afterwards: you're stuck with the 'acts of violence', stuck in realist abjection.

In a little time, as we get some distance from it, or even now, with a little imagination, it will be possible to read *La guerre du Golfe n'a pas eu lieu** as a science-fiction novel, as the anticipation, right in the thick of things, of the event as a fictional scenario – something into which it will surely be turned later. Like Borges' chronicling of cultures which never existed.

By making transparent the non-event of the war, you give it force in the imagination – somewhere other than in the 'real time' of news where it simply peters out. You give force to the illusion of war, rather than become an accessory to its false reality.

Anyhow, the book has fallen – quite logically – into the same black hole as the war. It has faded as quickly as the event whose absence it denounced. It was a successful non-event, like the Agency, like appearing on television. All this is as it should have been since it dealt with something which did not take place.

It was the *simulacrum of Helen* that was at the heart of the Trojan War. The Egyptian priests had held on to the original (we do not know what became of it) when she set out again with Paris for Troy. But, even without the magic of the priests, Helen was in any case merely a simulacrum, since the universal form of beauty is as unreal as gold, the universal form of all commodities. Every universal form is a simulacrum, since it is the simultaneous equivalent of all the others – something it is impossible for any real being to be.

There are many analogies between the Trojan and Gulf wars. Before the expedition, Menelaus called all the warriors of the Greek world to arms, just as Bush did with all the nations of the

* J. Baudrillard, Paris: Galileé, 1991.

'free world'. The incubation period of the war was very long (seven years in the case of Troy, seven months for the Gulf War) and the final phase was very rapid in both cases. The Greek victory was won at great cost to the victors, whom the gods punished relentlessly (the murder of Agamemnon, Clytaemnestra, Orestes, etc.). What will be the fate of the 'victors' of the Gulf War? Admittedly, this time the war did not take place. This difference leaves the Americans some hope, the gods having no real cause to avenge themselves.

If the Helen of the Trojan War was a simulacrum, what was the Gulf War's Helen? Where was there simulacrum here, *except in the simulacrum of war itself?*

Catastrophe management

The end of history, being itself a catastrophe, can only be fuelled by catastrophe. Managing the end therefore becomes synonymous with the management of catastrophe. And, quite specifically, of that catastrophe which is the slow extermination of the rest of the world.

We have long denounced the capitalistic, economic exploitation of the poverty of the 'other half of the world' [*l'autre monde*]. We must today denounce the moral and sentimental exploitation of that poverty – charity cannibalism being worse than oppressive violence. The extraction and humanitarian reprocessing of a destitution which has become the equivalent of oil deposits and gold mines. The extortion of the spectacle of poverty and, at the same time, of our charitable condescension: a worldwide appreciated surplus of fine sentiments and bad conscience. We should, in fact, see this not as the extraction of raw materials, but as a waste-reprocessing enterprise. Their destitution and our bad conscience are, in effect, all part of the waste-products of history – the main thing is to recycle them to produce a new energy source.

We have here an escalation in the psychological balance of terror. World capitalist oppression is now merely the vehicle and alibi for this other, much more ferocious, form of moral predation. One might almost say, contrary to the Marxist analysis, that material exploitation is only there to extract that spiritual raw material that is the misery of peoples, which serves as psychological nourishment for the rich countries and media nourishment for our daily lives.

The 'Fourth World' (we are no longer dealing with a 'developing' Third World) is once again beleaguered, this time as a catastrophe-bearing stratum. The West is whitewashed in the reprocessing of the rest of the world as waste and residue. And the white world repents and seeks absolution – it, too, the waste-product of its own history.

The South is a natural producer of raw materials, the latest of which is catastrophe. The North, for its part, specializes in the reprocessing of raw materials and hence also in the reprocessing of catastrophe. Bloodsucking protection, humanitarian interference, *Médecins sans frontières*, international solidarity, etc. The last phase of colonialism: the New Sentimental Order is merely the latest form of the New World Order. Other people's destitution becomes our adventure playground. Thus, the humanitarian offensive aimed at the Kurds – a show of repentance on the part of the Western powers after allowing Saddam Hussein to crush them – is in reality merely the second phase of the war, a phase in which charitable intervention finishes off the work of extermination. We are the consumers of the ever delightful spectacle of poverty and catastrophe, and of the moving spectacle of our own efforts to alleviate it (which, in fact, merely function to secure the conditions of reproduction of the catastrophe market); there, at least, in the order of moral profits, the Marxist analysis is wholly applicable: we see to it that extreme poverty is reproduced as a symbolic deposit, as a fuel essential to the moral and sentimental equilibrium of the West.

In our defence, it might be said that this extreme poverty was largely of our own making and it is therefore normal that we should profit by it.

There can be no finer proof that the distress of the rest of the world is at the root of Western power and that the spectacle of that distress is its crowning glory than the inauguration, on the roof of the *Arche de la Défense*, with a sumptuous buffet laid on by the *Fondation des Droits de l'homme*, of an exhibition of the finest photos of world poverty. Should we be surprised that spaces are set aside in the *Arche d'Alliance** for universal suffering hallowed by caviar and champagne?

Just as the economic crisis of the West will not be complete so long as it can still exploit the resources of the rest of the world, so the symbolic crisis will be complete only when it is no longer able to feed on the other half's human and natural catastrophes (Eastern Europe, the Gulf, the Kurds, Bangladesh, etc.). We need this drug, which serves us as an aphrodisiac and hallucinogen. And the poor countries are the best suppliers – as, indeed, they are of other drugs. We provide them, through our media, with the means to exploit this paradoxical resource, just as we give them the means to exhaust their natural resources with our technologies. Our whole culture lives off this catastrophic cannibalism, relayed in cynical mode by the news media, and carried forward in moral mode by our humanitarian aid, which is a way of encouraging it and ensuring its continuity, just as economic aid is a strategy for perpetuating under-development. Up to now, the financial sacrifice has been compensated a hundredfold by the moral gain. But when the catastrophe market itself reaches crisis point, in accordance with the implacable logic of the market, when distress becomes scarce or the marginal returns on it fall from overexploitation, when we run out of disasters from elsewhere or when they can no longer be traded like coffee or other commodities, the West will be forced to produce its own catastrophe for itself, in order to meet its need for spectacle and that voracious appetite for symbols which characterizes it even more than its voracious appetite for food. It will reach the point where it devours itself. When we have finished sucking out the destiny of others, we shall have to invent one for ourselves. The

---

* This is an allusion to the biblical '*Arche d'Alliance*' (the 'Ark of the Covenant'), as well as an ironic reference to the use here being made of the arch at La Défense.

Great Crash, the symbolic crash, will come in the end from us Westerners, but only when we are no longer able to feed on the hallucinogenic misery which comes to us from the other half of the world.

Yet they do not seem keen to give up their monopoly. The Middle East, Bangladesh, black Africa and Latin America are really going flat out in the distress and catastrophe stakes, and thus in providing symbolic nourishment for the rich world. They might be said to be overdoing it: heaping earthquakes, floods, famines and ecological disasters one upon another, and finding the means to massacre each other most of the time. The 'disaster show' goes on without any let-up and our sacrificial debt to them far exceeds their economic debt. The misery with which they generously overwhelm us is something we shall never be able to repay. The sacrifices we offer in return are laughable (a tornado or two, a few tiny holocausts on the roads, the odd financial sacrifice) and, moreover, by some infernal logic, these work out as much greater gains for us, whereas our kindnesses have merely added to the natural catastrophes another one immeasurably worse: the demographic catastrophe, a veritable epidemic which we deplore each day in pictures.

In short, there is such distortion between North and South, to the symbolic advantage of the South (a hundred thousand Iraqi dead against casualties numbered in tens on our side: in every case we are the losers), that one day everything will break down. One day, the West will break down if we are not soon washed clean of this shame, if an international congress of the poor countries does not very quickly decide to share out this symbolic privilege of misery and catastrophe. It is of course normal, since we refuse to allow the spread of nuclear weapons, that they should refuse to allow the spread of the catastrophe weapon. But it is not right that they should exert that monopoly indefinitely.

In any case, the under-developed are only so by comparison with the Western system and its presumed success. In the light of its assumed failure, they are not under-developed at all. They are only so in terms of a dominant evolutionism which has always been the worst of colonial ideologies. The argument here is that there is a line of objective progress and everyone is supposed to pass through its various stages (we find the same eyewash with regard to the evolution of species and in that evolutionism which unilaterally sanctions the superiority of the human race). In the light of current upheavals, which put an end to any idea of history as a linear process, there are no longer either developed or under-developed peoples. Thus, to encourage hope of evolution – albeit by revolution – among the poor and to doom them, in keeping with the objective illusion of progress, to technological salvation is a criminal absurdity. In actual fact, it is their good fortune to be able to escape from evolution just at the point when we no longer know where it is leading. In any case, a majority of these peoples, including those of Eastern Europe, do not seem keen to enter this evolutionist modernity, and their weight in the balance is certainly no small factor in the West's repudiation of its own history, of its own utopias and its own modernity. It might be said that the routes of violence, historical or otherwise, are being turned around and that the viruses now pass from South to North, there being every chance that, five hundred years after America was conquered, 1992 and the end of the century will mark the comeback of the defeated and the sudden reversal of that modernity.

The sense of pride is no longer on the side of wealth but of poverty, of those who – fortunately for them – have nothing to repent, and may indeed glory in being privileged in terms of catastrophes. Admittedly, this is a privilege they could hardly renounce, even if they wished to, but natural disasters merely reinforce the sense of guilt felt towards them by the wealthy – by those whom God visibly scorns since he no longer even strikes them down. One day it will be the Whites themselves who will give up their whiteness. It is a good bet that repentance will reach its highest pitch with the five-hundredth anniversary of the conquest of the Americas. We are going to have to lift the curse of the defeated – but symbolically victorious – peoples, which is insinuating itself five hundred years later, by way of repentance, into the heart of the white race.

No solution has been found to the dramatic situation of the under-developed, and none will be found since their drama has now been overtaken by that of the overdeveloped, of the rich nations. The psychodrama of congestion, saturation, super-abundance, neurosis and the breaking of blood vessels which haunts us – the drama of the excess of means over ends – calls more urgently for attention than that of penury, lack and poverty. That is where the most imminent danger of catastrophe resides, in the societies which have run out of emptiness.

Artificial catastrophes, like the beneficial aspects of civilization, progress much more quickly than natural ones. The under-developed are still at the primary stage of the natural, unforesee-able catastrophe. We are already at the second stage, that of the *manufactured* catastrophe – imminent and foreseeable – and we shall soon be at that of the *pre-programmed* catastrophe, the catastrophe of the third kind, deliberate and experimental. And, paradoxically, it is our pursuit of the means for averting natural catastrophe – the unpredictable form of destiny – which will take us there. Because it is unable to escape it, humanity will pretend to be the author of its destiny. Because it cannot accept being confronted with an end which is uncertain or governed by fate, it will prefer to stage its own death as a species.

The dance of the fossils

The fuelling of the end of history, which is proceeding by the recycling of wastes of all kinds, is also being achieved by reinjecting all the vestiges of a world without history. A truly species-wide sense of remorse is inducing humanity to resurrect the whole of its past just when it is losing the thread of its memory. All the relics, all the traces which were shrouded in the greatest secrecy and which, by that token, formed part of our symbolic capital, will be exhumed and resuscitated: they will not be spared our transparency; we shall turn them from something buried and living into something visible and dead; we shall turn their symbolic capital into a folkloric, museum capital. Palaeontology reigns, it would seem, over a kind of criminal unconscious of the species, since this race for fossils, this forced exploration bears a strange resemblance to the exploring of the fossils of the unconscious. Each has about it the same *ressentiment* as to our origins, the same original repentance, an identical vague sense of criminal responsibility towards our ancestors and our fantasies.

Nothing disappears, nothing must disappear: that is the watchword of this new therapeutic overzealousness, the overzealousness of memory and archaeology.* A hypertelic memory

---

* The notion of *acharnement thérapeutique*, here translated as 'therapeutic overzealousness', has been at the centre of recent debates in France on the lengths to which doctors should properly go to keep patients alive, especially where life expectancy is short.

which stores all data in a constant state of instant retrievability, excluding any work of mourning, any resolution of the past. The Unconscious is already something of this kind. It knows neither past nor forgetting, is neither archaic nor archaeological. It is, indeed, on the contrary, a perpetual present, an instantaneousness of all psychic events, which show on its surface in a continual, potential *passage à l'acte*. Paradoxically, by dint of this zealous effort forcibly to bring back into the present what we no longer even remember, we live in a world which is both without memory and without forgetting. This is what heaven – or hell – must be like: the massive recall, at every moment, of all the patterns of our life. The penitentiary immortality, the carceral immortality of an unrelenting memory.

If modernity, in its day, gave rise to anthropological exploration, post-modernity, for its part, has spawned a positive craze for the neolithic and the paleolithic. The extraction of relics has become an industrial undertaking. And it is, indeed, the great modern construction projects (high-speed trains, motorways, city development) which keep these archaeological finds coming. Palaeontology is advancing at the same pace as the latest technology. Sites, relics, tools and bones: a whole stratum of signs, many thousands of years old, wrested back from oblivion. Thus, technology can pride itself on enriching the cultural heritage at the same time as it is destroying the territory.

Ironically, we might say that we are watching the liberation of fossils, just like everything else. Bercy, Silumian, Cassis, the dugouts, the bones, the wall paintings – relics are everywhere rushing to be discovered. They too want to express themselves. They have waited too long. This is not like America, which had no wish to be discovered at all, but the outcome is the same: everything discovered is wiped out. The fossils return from their immemoriality, and thus from humanity's secret memories, only to be immediately buried again in its artificial ones. No sooner exhumed than sequestered. All the originals are put under lock and key (the Lascaux caves, the Tautavel skull, the underwater cave at Cassis). More and more things are exhumed to be immediately reinterred, snatched from death only to be cryogenized in perpetuity. Defence secrets: the underwater entrance to the Cassis cave was blocked up by the Navy and, in the same operation, the site scheduled a monument by the Ministry of Culture. A dismal attempt to sequester a collective memory that is everywhere on the slide. Thousands of works of art already slumber in safes, keeping the art market afloat. A striking demonstration that the abstraction of value is based on the subtraction of enjoyment. Even abstract forms, ideas and concepts lie deep-frozen in the sanctuaries of Memory and Artificial Intelligence. As with Lascaux, only copies, photos, duplicates are placed in circulation. The Xerox degree of culture. In its way, Biosphere 2 is also an attempt ideally to sequester the species and its environment behind the crystal curtain of the forbidden gaze, the forbidden touch, safe from all real lusts of the flesh and prey to a definitive fetishism.

Not only does this archaeological fetishism condemn its objects to become museological waste, a phenomenon contemporaneous with industrial waste, it also betrays a suspect nostalgia. It is because we are moving further and further away from our history that we are avid for signs of the past, not, by any means, in order to resuscitate them, but to fill up the empty space of our memories. Or perhaps man, in the process of losing track of his history, is seized by a nostalgia for societies without history, perhaps obscurely sensing that he is returning to the same point. All these relics which we call upon to bear witness to our origin would then become the involuntary signs of its loss.

When faced with the cave paintings, the people of the eighteenth century would not believe in them. They saw them as a mystification got up by libertines to mock the Bible (it was said the caves had been painted to make people believe in a humanity antedating Christ). Today when, for want of any faith in Revelation, we require a certificate of origin, we are *too* keen to believe in them. If these relics did not exist, they would have to be invented. All is explained by our unsated desire for authenticity, by the poverty of imagination of our modern societies. This explains why we cannot even pose the question of their authenticity since, even if true, they seem invented to satisfy the needs of the anthropological cause, to meet the superstitious demand for an 'objective' proof of our origin duly certified by carbon 14. In fact, their being discovered wrenches them instantly from their truth and secrecy to freeze them in the universe of museums, where they are no longer either true or false, but verified by a scientific fetishism which is an accessory to our fetishistic will to believe in them. In this respect they share the fate of many other things in our culture: arguments, works, events themselves have no other credibility than that deriving from their price on the imaginary stock-exchange of values.

Our reasons for authenticating these relics are as unobjective as the eighteenth-century reasons for denying their authenticity. Then, they were seen as true simulacra. We accord them a false authenticity or, rather, a value which is indeterminable, since our desires play a part in it. Like those objects Freud speaks of, which, because they are closest to the female sexual organs, play that role in sexual hallucinations, we fetishize fossils and relics because they are closest to the lost origin and stand in for us as hallucinations of an origin. In fact, just as fetish objects conceal the refusal of difference and sexual *jouissance*, so the cult of fossils conceals a form of *ressentiment* and of deep disavowal of the origin and the original secret.

Besides, we immediately substitute a copy – the only version appropriate to our universe, where every original constitutes a potential danger and all singularity runs the risk of hindering the free circulation of value – thus, for example, Numa made twelve copies of the sacred shield, one for each tribe of Rome, and destroyed the original. We are not far from doing the same when we lock away the Tautavel skull in a bank vault or open up the simulacrum of the Lascaux cave to the public (we shall no doubt soon have to close the second cave, an exact replica of the first; it seems that simulacra decay even more quickly than the originals.

We ought to think about building a third or a fourth version, at which point the present copy would immediately take on historical value). The fact that we are reduced to gazing at copies admittedly betrays the most profound contempt both for these objects and for ourselves. But, where reality is concerned, we have long contented ourselves with images, and where things are concerned, with copies. We secretly prefer not to be confronted with the original any longer. All we want is the copyright.

Apart from the doubt automatically attaching to anything which turns up so wonderfully on cue (be it relics, scientific discoveries or historical events), and to anything which is, to some extent, invented by our own gaze, another anxiety arises where this enterprise of resurrecting all traces is concerned. Are we trapped in an exhaustive, obsessional recollection of all the moments the species has lived through? In a revival of all previous phases? In the detailed reconstruction of what would then seem like a crime (the appearance of life and the human race on earth), since it is only with crimes that such a relentless reconstitution is mounted? Is the whole of the future going to exhaust itself in the artificial synthesizing of the past? Who knows where this gigantic backward movement is leading? Is it an ephemeral phase in our post-history and therefore a cultural phenomenon, or a development of much profounder import, relating to the fate of the species or even, beyond that, to oscillations of a cosmic type? (With the tadpole, once the high point of sexuation is reached, there is involution towards earlier forms of reproduction. Might human beings be reinventing biological cloning at the end-point of a sexed history? Death drive or a pulsation of a cosmic type?)

At all events, this mass resurgence of fossils and relics is troubling, as troubling as the signs which used to appear in the sky presaging great events. We should be wary of all these phantoms ripped from their tombs. The information they provide about our past is a mask and I can already hear their sarcastic laughter. When our past has been exhumed, when all that had disappeared has reappeared, the dead will outnumber the living and there will be the same imbalance as will come about when there is more computing matter [*substance informatique*] and artificial intelligence on earth than natural intelligence. Then we shall be cast into sidereal space, the space of networks, or into fossil space, the space of the kingdom of the dead . . .

Maleficent ecology

The worst of it is that, in the course of this universal recycling of waste, which has become our historic task, the human race is beginning to produce itself as waste-product, to carry out this work of waste disposal on itself. What is worst is not that we are submerged by the waste-products of industrial and urban concentration, but that *we ourselves are transformed into residues.* Nature – the natural world – is becoming residual, insignificant, an encumbrance, and we do not know how to dispose of it. By producing highly centralized structures, highly developed urban, industrial and technical systems, by remorselessly condensing down programmes, functions and models, we are transforming all the rest into waste, residues, useless relics. By putting the higher functions into orbit, we are transforming the planet itself into a waste-product, a marginal territory, a peripheral space. Building a motorway, a hypermarket or a metropolis automatically means transforming all that surrounds it into desert. Creating ultra-rapid communication networks immediately means transforming human exchange into a residue. The example of Biosphere 2 is an eloquent one: in the image of ideal synthesis it wishes to provide of our planet, in its character as experimental artifact, it is a way of transforming our environment into an archaic residue, to be tipped into the dustbins of natural history.

As for the dustbins of history themselves, they are not so much full of events or outdated ideologies as of present events, immediately voided of their meaning by news, transformed into crusher residues, into a charnel-house of images. News is the excremental production of the event as waste; it is the current dustbin of history. There is nothing to counter the implacable rule which states that the virtual produces the real as its waste-product. No ecology – no benevolent ecology – can do anything to stop it. It would take a maleficent ecology – one which treats evil with evil.

Moreover, waste is today produced as such. We build huge office spaces which are intended to remain eternally empty (the spaces, like the people, are 'laid off'). We put up buildings that are still-born, remnants which will never have been anything but remnants (our age no longer produces ruins or relics, only wastes and residues). Genuine monuments to disaffection with the human project, insofar as all that was asked of them was to provide employment, to keep the economic wheels turning for the time required by their useless construction. Perhaps it is they which stand as true testimony to this civilization – commemorating within its own lifetime an industrial and bureaucratic system that is already dead? Here again, history is taking a fantastic step backwards by building the ruins of the future, the ruins of an apparatus which continues to grow like a virtual waste-product. One can imagine entire towns put together not from the wastes of what has already served a purpose and therefore retained some trace of its previous usage, but of things that were waste 'from the outset' (this is already the case with generations of missiles, and with industrial plant and real estate), assured of never growing old or being revived in any memory – the phantoms of breakneck investment and even more rapid disinvestment.

The production of waste *as waste* is accompanied by its idealization and its promotion in advertising. It is the same with the production of *man* as waste-product, which is accompanied by his being idealized and promoted in the form of human rights. Idealization always goes with abjection, just as charity always goes with destitution. This is a kind of symbolic rule. A new wave of human-beings-as-waste ('boat people', deportees, the dis-appeared, 'ghost-people' of all kinds) is accompanied by a new human rights offensive.

Hence the recent proposal, following this same logic, from the moment it achieved the status of virtual waste-product, to accord nature international recognition of its rights, to elevate it to the status of a subject in law. Thus the *'contrat naturel'** amounts to a definitive recognition of nature as waste. Just as, in bygone days, the recognition of the rights of the unfortunate meant not their emancipation as citizens, but their liberation as the unfortunate.

It is always the same with rights: the right to water, the right to air, the right to existence, etc. It is when all these fine things have disappeared that the law arrives to grant their disappearance official recognition. The law is like religious faith. If God exists, there is no need to believe in Him. If people do believe in Him, this is because the self-evidence of his existence has passed away. Thus, when people obtain the right to life, the fact is that they are no longer able to live. When nature is recognized as a subject in law, as it is by Michel Serres, we have objectified it to death, and this ecological cover merely asserts our right to go on doing so.

All this has been brought about by the highly dubious way in which the concept of nature has evolved. What was initially matter became energy. The modern discovery of nature consists in its liberation as energy and in a mechanical transformation of the world. After having first been matter, and then energy, nature is today becoming an interactive subject. It is ceasing to be an object, but this is bringing it all the more surely into the circuit of subjection. A dramatic paradox, and one which also affects human beings: we are much more compromised when we cease to be objects and become subjects. This is a trick that was pulled on us long ago, in the name of absolute liberation. Let's not pull the same one on nature. For the ultimate danger is that, in an interactivity built up into a total system of communication, there is no *other*; there are only subjects – and, very soon, only subjects without objects. All our problems today as civilized beings

* A reference to the title of a work by Michel Serres.

originate here: not in an excess of alienation, but a disappearance of alienation in favour of a maximum transparency between subjects. An unbearable situation, all the more so for the fact that, in foisting on nature the status of a subject in law, we are also foisting on it all the vices of subjectivity, decking it out, in our own image, with a bad conscience, with nostalgia (for a lost object which, in this case, can only be *us*), with a range of drives – in particular, an impulse for revenge. The 'balance' we hear so much of in ecology ('out of balance') is not so much that of planetary resources and their exploitation as the metaphysical one between subject and object. Now, that metaphysical subject/object balance is being upset and the subject, armed as he is with all the technologies of advanced communication (technologies on whose horizon the object has disappeared), is the beneficiary. Once that balance is disrupted, it inevitably sparks violent reactions on the part of the object. Just as individuals counter the transparency and virtual responsibility inflicted on them as subjects with unexplainable acts, acts of resistance, failure, delinquency and collective disorder, so nature counters this enforced promotion, this consensual, communicational black-mail, with various forms of behaviour that are radically other, such as catastrophes, upheavals, earthquakes and chaos. It would seem that nature does not really feel a sense of responsibility for itself, nor does it react to our efforts to give it one. We are, admittedly, indulging in a (bad) ecological conscience and attempting, by this moral violence, to stave off possible violence on nature's part. But if, by offering it the status of subject, we are handing it the same poisoned chalice as we gave to the decolonized nations, we ought not to be surprised if it behaves irrationally merely so as to assert itself as such. Contrary to the underlying Rousseauist ideology, which argues that the profound nature of the liberated subject can only be good and that nature itself, once emancipated, cannot but be endowed with natural equilibrium and all the ecological virtues, there is nothing more ambiguous or perverse than a subject. Now, nature is also germs, viruses, chaos, bacteria and scorpions, significantly eliminated from Biosphere 2 as though they were not meant to exist. Where are the deadly little scorpions, so beautiful and so translucent, which one sees in the Desert Museum not far away, scorpions whose magical sting certainly performs a higher, invisible – but necessary – function within our Biosphere 1: the incarnation of evil, of the venomous evil of chance, the mortal innocence of desire (the desire for death) in the equilibrium of living beings?

What they have forgotten is that what binds living beings together is something other than an ecological, biospherical solidarity, something other than the homeostatic equilibrium of a system: it is the cycle of metamorphoses. Man is also a scorpion, just as the Bororo are *araras* and, left to himself in an expurgated universe, he becomes, himself, a scorpion.*

In short, it is not by expurgating evil that we liberate good. Worse, by liberating good, we also liberate evil. And this is only right: it is the rule of the symbolic game. It is the inseparability of good and evil which constitutes our true equilibrium, our true balance. We ought not to entertain the illusion that we might separate the two, that we might cultivate good and happiness in a pure state and expel evil and sorrow as wastes. That is the terroristic dream of the transparency of good, which very quickly ends in its opposite, the transparency of evil.

We must not reconcile ourselves with nature.

It seems that the more the human race reconciles itself with nature, the less it is reconciled with itself. Above and beyond the violence it inflicts on others, there is a violence specific to the human race in general, a violence of the species against itself in which it treats itself as a residue, as a survivor – even in the present – of a coming catastrophe. As if it too were ready to repent of an evolution which has brought it such privileges and carried it to such extremes. This is the same conjuncture as the one to which Canetti refers, in which we stepped out of history, except that here we have not stepped out of history, but have passed a point beyond which *nothing is either human or inhuman*

* *Arara* is a name of Tupi origin for a bird of the genus *Ara* which includes the macaws (French: *aras*).

any longer and what is at stake, which is even more immense, is the tottering of the species into the void.

It is quite possible that, in this process, the species itself is commencing its own disappearance, either by disenchantment with – or *ressentiment* towards – itself, or out of a deliberate inclination which leads it here and now to manage that disappearance as its destiny.

Surreptitiously, in spite of our superiority (or perhaps because of it), we are carrying over on to our own species the treatment we mete out to the others, all of which are virtually dying out. In an animal milieu which has reached saturation point, species are spontaneously dissuaded from living. The effects produced by the finite nature of the earth, for the first time contrasting violently with the infinity of our development, are such that our species is automatically switching over to collective suicide. Whether by external (nuclear) violence or internal (biological) virulence. We are subjecting ourselves as a human species to the same experimental pressure as the animal species in our laboratories.

Man is without prejudice: he is using himself as a guinea-pig, just as he is using the rest of the world, animate or inanimate. He is cheerfully gambling with the destiny of his own species as he is with that of all the others. In his blind desire to know more, he is programming his own destruction with the same ease and ferocity as the destruction of the others. He cannot be accused of a superior egoism. He is sacrificing himself, as a species, to *an unknown experimental fate*, unknown at least as yet to other species, who have experienced only natural fates. And, whereas it seemed that, linked to that natural fate, there was something like an instinct of self-preservation – long the mainstay of a natural philosophy of individuals and groups – this experimental fate to which the human species is condemning itself by unprecedented, artificial means, this scientific prefiguring of its own disappearance, sweeps away all ideas of a self-preservation instinct. The idea is, indeed, no longer discussed in the human sciences (where the focus of attention would seem, rather, to be on the death drive) and this disappearance from the field of thought signals that, beneath a frenzy for ecological conservation which is really more to do with nostalgia and remorse, a wholly different tendency has already won out, the sacrificing of the species to boundless experimentation.

A contradictory dual operation: man, alone of all species, is seeking to construct his immortal double, an unprecedented artificial species. He caps natural selection with an artificial super-selection, claiming sole possession of a soul and a consciousness and, at the same time, he is putting an end to natural selection which entailed the death of each species in accordance with the law of evolution. In ending evolution (of all species including his own), he is contravening the symbolic rule and hence truly deserves to disappear. And this is without doubt the destiny he is preparing for himself, in a roundabout way, in that, in his arrogant desire to end evolution, man is ushering in *involution* and the revival of inhuman, biogenetic forms. Here again, we have before us a reversive effect, running counter to any ideal or 'scientific' vision of the species.

The idea running through the writings of Darwin that natural selection leads to a species capable of morally transcending natural selection is thoroughly specious. In aiming for virtual (technical) immortality and ensuring its exclusive perpetuation by a projection into artifacts, the human species is precisely losing its own immunity and specificity and becoming immortalized *as an inhuman species*; it is abolishing in itself the mortality of the living in favour of the immortality of the dead. It is immortalizing itself as the zero degree of a living species, as an operational artifact which no longer even obeys the law of species, except the law of artificial species, whose mortality is perhaps even more rapid. As a result, by going down these paths of artifice which were supposed to ensure its indefinite survival, it is perhaps hurtling even more quickly to its doom.

The human species is currently domesticating itself, this time for good, by means of its technologies. It is submitting collectively to the same rituals as insects. Soon it will submit to the same controlled techniques of reproduction as the protozoa, will inflict on itself the same biogenetic (phylo- or ontogenetic) destiny to which it has subjected others. It no longer, in fact, sees itself as different from the others, in spite of its supremacy. It treats itself as a species that may be ruthlessly exploited, condemned to a brutalization and annihilation of its own. Here again, all the advances it has made and has forced others to accept have had a reversive effect upon it. To such an extent that it – the guardian, in its zoos, museums, reserves and laboratories, of condemned species – regards itself as a condemned species, and keeps an anxious eye trained on its biospheric destiny.

The finest example of what the human species is capable of inflicting upon itself is Biosphere 2 – the first zoological gardens of the species, to which human beings come to watch themselves survive, as once they went to watch apes copulate. Outside Tucson, in Arizona, right in the middle of the desert, a geodesic glass and metal structure accommodating all the planet's climates in miniature, where eight human beings (four men and four women, of course) are to live self-sufficiently, in a closed circuit, for two years, in order – since we are not able to change our lives – to explore the conditions for our survival. A minimal representation of the species in an experimental situation, in a kind of spaceship allegory. As a museum mock-up of the future, but of an unpredictable future – a century hence, a thousand years, millions . . . who knows? – it forms a pendant to the Desert Museum some sixty miles away, which retraces the geological and animal history of two hundred million years. The point of convergence between the two being the idea of the conservation and optimal management of residues – of the relics of the past for the Desert Museum, the anticipated relics of the future for Biosphere 2 – not to mention the magical desert site which allows the problem of survival to be examined, both that of nature and that of the species with equal rigour.

Such a very American hallucination this ocean, this savannah, this desert, this virgin forest reconstituted in miniature, vitrified beneath their experimental bubble. In the true spirit of Disneyland's attractions, Biosphere 2 is not an experiment, but an experimental attraction. The most amazing thing is that they have reconstituted a fragment of artificial desert right in the middle of the natural desert (a bit like reconstituting Hollywood in Disneyworld). Only in this artificial desert there are neither scorpions nor Indians to be exterminated; there are only extraterrestrials trained to survive in the very place where they destroyed another, far better adapted race, leaving it no chance.

The whole humanist ideology – ecological, climatic, micro-cosmic and biogenetic – is summed up here, but this is of no importance. Only the sidereal, transparent form of the edifice means anything – but what? Difficult to say. As ever, absolute space inspires engineers, gives meaning to a project which has none, except the mad desire for a miniaturization of the human species, with a view perhaps to a future race and its emergence, of which we still dream . . .

The artificial promiscuity of climates has its counterpart in the artificial immunity of the space: the elimination of all spontaneous generation (of germs, viruses, microbes), the automatic purifica-tion of the water, the air, the physical atmosphere (and the mental atmosphere too, purified by science). The elimination of all sexual reproduction: it is forbidden to reproduce in Biosphere 2; even contamination from life [*le vivant*] is dangerous; sexuality may spoil the experiment. Sexual difference functions only as a formal, statistical variable (the same number of women as men; if anyone drops out, a person of the same sex is substituted).

Everything here is designed with a brain-like abstraction. Biosphere 2 is to Biosphere 1 (the whole of our planet and the cosmos) what the brain is to the human being in general: the synthesis in miniature of all its possible functions and operations: the desert lobe, the virgin forest lobe, the nourishing agriculture lobe, the residential lobe, all carefully distinct and placed side by side, according to the analytical imperative. All of this in reality entirely outdated with respect to what we now know about the brain – its plasticity, its elasticity, the reversible sequencing of all its operations. There is, then, behind this archaic model, beneath its futuristic exterior, a gigantic hypothetical error, a fierce idealization doomed to failure.

In fact, the 'truth' of the operation lies elsewhere, and you sense this when you return from Biosphere 2 to 'real' America, as you do when you emerge from Disneyland into real life: the fact is that the imaginary, or experimental, model is in no way different from the real functioning of this society. Just as the whole of America is built in the image of Disneyland, so the whole of American society is carrying on – in real time and out in the open – the same experiment as Biosphere 2 which is therefore only falsely experimental, just as Disneyland is only falsely imaginary. The recycling of all substances, the integration of flows and circuits, non-pollution, artificial immunity, ecological balancing, controlled abstinence, restrained *jouissance* but, also, the right of all species to survival and conservation – and not just plant and animal species, but also social ones. All categories formally brought under the one umbrella of the law – this latter setting its seal on the ending of natural selection.

It is generally thought that the obsession with survival is a logical consequence of life and the right to life. But, most of the time, the two things are contradictory. Life is not a question of rights, and what follows on from life is not survival, which is artificial, but death. It is only by paying the price of a failure to live, a failure to take pleasure, a failure to die that man is assured of survival. At least in present conditions, which the Biosphere principle perpetuates.

This micro-universe seeks to exorcize catastrophe by making an artificial synthesis of all the elements of catastrophe. From the perspective of survival, of recycling and feedback, of stabilization and metastabilization, the elements of life are sacrificed to those of survival (elimination of germs, of evil, of sex). Real life, which surely, after all, has the right to disappear (or might there be a paradoxical limit to human rights?), is sacrificed to artificial survival. The real planet, presumed condemned, is sacrificed in advance to its miniaturized, air-conditioned clone (have no fear, all the earth's climates are air-conditioned here) which is designed to vanquish death by total simulation. In days gone by it was the dead who were embalmed for eternity; today, it is the living we embalm alive in a state of survival. Must this be our hope?

Having lost our metaphysical utopias, do we have to build this prophylactic one?

What, then, is this species endowed with the insane pretension to survive – not to transcend itself by virtue of its natural intelligence, but to survive physically, biologically, by virtue of its artificial intelligence? Is there a species destined to escape natural selection, natural disappearance – in a word, death? What cosmic cussedness might give rise to such a turnabout? What vital reaction might produce the idea of survival at any cost? What metaphysical anomaly might grant the right not to disappear – logical counterpart of the remarkable good fortune of having appeared? There is a kind of aberration in the attempt to eternalize the species – not to immortalize it in its actions, but to eternalize it in this face-lifted coma, in the glass coffin of Biosphere 2.

We may, nonetheless, take the view that this experiment, like any attempt to achieve artificial survival or artificial paradise, is illusory, not from any technical shortcomings, but in its very principle. In spite of itself, it is threatened by the same accidents as real life. Fortunately. Let us hope that the random universe outside smashes this glass coffin. Any accident will do if it rescues us from a scientific euphoria sustained by drip-feed.

Immortality

Curiously, all the assumptions, explicit or implicit, of Biosphere 2 link up with the issues raised in the Middle Ages by the problems of immortality and resurrection. Would bodies resuscitate with all their organs (including the sexual ones), with their illnesses, their distinctive features, with all that made them specific living beings? We might widen the question today by asking whether we shall resuscitate with our desires, our wants, our neuroses, our unconscious, our alienation? With our handicaps, our viruses, our manias? In its simulation of ideal resurrection, with all negative features eliminated, Biosphere 2 provides answers to all these questions. No viruses, no germs, no scorpions, no reproduction. Everything is expurgated, idealized, immunized, immortalized by transparency, disincarnation, disinfection and prophylaxis – exactly as in paradise. Moreover, if the medieval theologians were close to heresy when they enquired into the concrete forms of the resurrection of bodies, the officials at Biosphere 2 certainly make you feel any half-way detailed examination of the conditions of the experiment betokens the most evil intent.

What is being set in place here is, in effect, the immortality of the species *in real time*. We long ago stopped believing in the immortality of the soul, a deferred immortality. We no longer believe in that immortality which assumed a transcending of the end, an intense investment in the finalities of the beyond and a symbolic elaboration of death. What we want is the immediate realization of immortality by all possible means. At this millennium end, we have all, in fact, become millenarian: we desire the immediate attainment of existence without end, just as the medieval millenarians wanted paradise in real time – God's Kingdom on earth.

But we want this immortality here and now, this real-time afterlife, *without having resolved the problem of the end*. For there is no real-time end, no real time of death. This is an absurdity. The end is always experienced after it has actually happened, in its symbolic elaboration. It follows from this that real-time immortality is itself an *absurdity* (whereas imagined immortality was not: it was an *illusion*). Biosphere 2 is an absurdity. For, at bottom, *nothing takes place in real time*. Not even history. History in real time is CNN, instant news, which is the exact opposite of history. But this is precisely our fantasy of passing beyond the end, of emancipating ourselves from time. And the CNN presenter locked away in his studio at the virtual centre of the world is the homologue of his Bio 2 brothers and sisters. They have all passed over into real time, the one into the real time of events, the others into real-time survival. And, of course, into the same unreality.

It is doubtless because it has not been able to resolve the problem of the end (quite simply because it is insoluble) that humanity has turned its attention to the beginning. We have, so to speak, shifted our sights from the final conditions to the initial ones; we have moved from a vision of things in terms of their final state to a vision in terms of their genesis. Not in the sense of Genesis, of course, but in the sense of their being determined by their origin, of everything following a genetic sequence and being genetically manipulable. Against the illusion of the end and of final determinations, truth has become the truth of what precedes. The illusion of the end has been supplanted by the illusion of the cause. In this perspective, there is no place for a finalistic conception of immortality. We can no more think in terms of the immortality of the soul or the stars than Kepler could avoid thinking in those terms. For him, that finality seemed entirely obvious; for us the very opposite seems entirely obvious.

In this genetic order – or random disorder – which is ours, there is no longer any place for a finalistic conception of anything whatever. No end is conceivable, not even the end of history. We are reduced to working on what happens beyond the end, on technical immortality, without having passed through death, through the symbolic elaboration of the end.

One can only arrive at a clear conception of immortality in a stable, unchanging universe. In a universe where a divine sanction ensures the eternity of the cosmic order (Kepler's universe), immortality is akin to a natural property of the human micro-cosm. It is merely the logical extension of the continuity of an order. The universe could not change since all is ordained by a higher decree. By contrast, as soon as that order begins to break up, as soon as that transcendence is lost, the cosmic order, like the human order, emancipated from God and all finality, becomes shifting and unstable; it falls prey to entropy, to the final dissipation of energy, and death. The happy consciousness of eternity and immortality is ended. The problem of the end becomes crucial and insoluble. *There will no longer be an end*. We enter upon a kind of radical indeterminacy. For not only is the transcendent finality lost, it turns against itself, loses itself in upheavals, and even disrupts causes and the course of events. For all we might strive to forget the problem of the end, then, or circumvent it by artificial technical solutions, the end does not forget us.

So long as there is a finalistic conception of life and death, the soul, the afterlife and immortality are given, like the world, and there is no cause to believe in them. Do you believe in reality [*le réel*]? No, of course not: it exists but we do not believe in it. It is like God. Do you believe in God? No, of course not: God exists, but I don't believe in him. To wager that God exists and to believe in him – or that he doesn't exist and not to believe in him – is of such banality as almost to make us doubt the question, while the two propositions 'God exists, but I don't believe in him' and 'God doesn't exist, but I believe in him' both, paradoxically, suggest that, if God exists, there is no need to believe in him, but that if he does not exist, there is every need to believe in him. If something does not exist, you have to believe in it. Belief is not the reflection of existence, *it is there for existence*, just as language is not the reflection of meaning, it is there in place of meaning.

To believe in God is, therefore, to doubt his existence, his manifestness, his presence. It is to have a need to appeal to him, to produce him, to bear subjective witness to him. Now, why, if he exists, does he need our witness? This amounts almost to thinking that God only exists by an impulse of the spirit, which is not far removed from blasphemy. In fact, faith is the spiritual impulse which reveals the profoundest uncertainty about the existence of God (but it is the same with all the theological virtues: hope is the spiritual impulse which betrays the deepest despair at the real state of things and charity the spiritual impulse which betrays the deepest contempt for others).

Belief is superfluous, just as Canetti says vengeance is super-fluous; it is rendered unnecessary by the inexorable reversibility of things. In exactly the same way, passion is a useless supplement to the natural attraction between beings, and we might say the same of truth, which merely complicates appearances unnecessar-ily. Belief is, then, merely an unnecessary complication of the question of the existence or non-existence of God. God, for his part, if he exists, does not believe in his existence, but he allows the subject to believe in it, and to believe he believes in it, or not to believe that – but not to believe he does not believe in it (Stravogin). Impenetrable labyrinth of belief, today broken down by the dissipation of the very notion of reality. It is no longer a question today of believing or not believing in the images which pass before our eyes. We refract reality and signs indifferently without believing in them. This is not even incredulity: our images simply pass through our brains without landing on the square marked 'belief', just as we pass through the political space without landing on the square marked 'representation'. We merely refract the illusion of the political, in the same way as news merely refracts the media illusion of events (it does not, itself, believe in them), or as a mirror merely refracts your image without believing in it.

As for credibility, which has taken the place of belief, it is a property not of the subject but of the object. It is the object which is credible. Or rather, if belief still presupposes an (imaginary) relation between subject and object, credibility, for its part, merely supposes a relation between the object and the code. This is an important new twist, since it reflects what has also happened to immortality, which is no longer for us today a property of the subject but of the biological process.

It is when immortality becomes an object of belief, when God, the soul, the afterlife and resurrection cease to be radical illusions and become objects of belief that they fall prey, by that same token, to philosophical critique. That critique does not attack the radical illusion, but a representation and a belief – that is, a relation already weakened by its ambiguity. It is because there is, in belief, an internal contest with incredulity that it becomes a vulnerable target and one tailor-made for philosophical criticism (that is why, in our view, the critique of the notion of belief is, in substance, ended, just as Marx said religion was ended: one must either cleave to radical illusion or radical indifference, eliminating the intermediate forms of belief).

It is in his *Gedanken über Tod und Unsterblichkeit* [Thoughts on death and immortality] that Feuerbach undertakes the deconstruction of all this religious configuration of the afterlife, the immortality of the soul and resurrection. For the human race, this emancipation from all superstition signifies the recovery of its lost essence. But what will the human race do once free of any belief? It will either fulfil itself egoistically, obeying an exclusive, sovereign individualism (Stirner), or do so collectively, by setting out on a long, historical course, as in Marx, or it will shift its sights to the Superhuman, through a transvaluation of the values of the species – this is the path marked out by Nietzsche, who argued that the human race cannot be left to itself, but must aim beyond itself and discover the great metamorphosis — that of becoming.

All these bodies of thought have had profound consequences for our world — none has turned itself into a reality. Each aims for an ideal transfiguration and allots a sovereign goal to the emancipated human race, aspiring to a 'beyond' which is no longer that of religion, but a 'beyond' of the human which remains *within* the human, humanity reaching beyond its own condition, achieving a transcendence which arises out of its own capacities — an illusion perhaps, but a superior illusion.

Nietzsche has written magnificently of the vital illusion — not that of 'worlds beyond' [*arrière-mondes*], but the illusion of appearances, of the forms of becoming, of the veil and, indeed, all the veils which, happily, protect us from the objective illusion, the illusion of truth, from the transparent relation of the world to an objective truth, from the transparent relation of man to his own truth. This is the illusion of meaning, secreted by man when he takes himself to be the subject of history and the world. To which we can only oppose the *illusion of the world itself*, whose rules, admittedly mysterious and arbitrary, are nonetheless immanent and necessary. Contrary to the transcendent illusion of religions, the play of appearances is superhuman, which is to say that the human race can only attain sovereignty by a transvaluation of values; otherwise, it remains condemned to superstitious beliefs of all kinds, including the more modern ones of psychology and technology, including the superstitious belief in itself as the definitive species. Not immortal by glory, but definitive by the mastery of survival, by technical fetishism, by a domestication of itself which is merely the parody of the acceptance of its fate, by a biological manipulation which is merely the caricature of the transvaluation of values.

Needless to say, this transvaluation of values of which Nietzsche speaks has not taken place, except precisely in the opposite sense — *not beyond, but this side of, good and evil*, not beyond, but this side of, true and false, beautiful and ugly, etc. A transvaluation folding in upon itself towards a non-differentiation, a non-distinction of values, itself fetishized in an aesthetics of plurality, of difference, etc. Not any longer a fetishization of divinities, great ideas or grand narratives, but of minimal differences and particles. It is in this respect that fetishism has become radical: it has become minimal and molecular; it is no longer the fetishism of a *form*, but of a mere *formula* – subliminal, subhuman. The boundaries of the human and the inhuman are indeed blurring, yet they are doing so in a movement not towards the super-human, but towards the subhuman, towards a disappearance of the very symbolic characteristics of the species. *Verklärung des Untermenschen*. Transfiguration of the subman.

What is currently taking place in transmutation's stead is a transcription of the Idea – including that of immortality – into its technical operation, a transcription of the human race itself into an immortal, artificial species, ensuring its genetic and generic survival by all available means. Which shows Nietzsche in one sense to be right: the human race, left to itself, is in fact only able to reduplicate or destroy itself.

Not just by destroying its environment and its biological substratum, but by destroying its symbolic space and, more specifically, every vital illusion – the illusion of appearances, ideas, dreams, utopias, ideal projections, but also the illusion of concepts and representations, including those of death and of the body, which is disappearing more and more – as a result of the immediate effectuation of all these things instead of their symbolic elaboration. Destruction by unconditional actualization of all that was formerly merely a dream, a myth, an ideality, an appearance and which – whether destined to remain so or not – formed part of the symbolic equilibrium of life and death.

This de-differentiation of the human and the inhuman, this reabsorption of the metaphor of life into the metastasis of survival is effected by a progressive reduction to the lowest common denominator. At the level of genes, the genome and the genotype, the signs distinctive of humanity are fading; at least, they no longer have symbolic value, but merely a functional pur-pose. No more transfiguration, no more metaphors: immortality has passed over into the (biological, genetic) code, the only immortal token which remains, the only feature immortalized in living matter. We have the perpetual motion of the code, the metonymic eternity of cells. Generation by formulas, algebraic or genetic, has everywhere supplanted the play and destiny of forms. The worst thing is that the living beings generated by formula will not outlive their own formulas; they are therefore, from the outset, living on borrowed time.

Paradoxically, it is the irruption of biology, that is, of the science of life, which marks this irruption of the non-living, marks an end to the transcending of the non-living by the living. Just as the irruption of psychology marks the end of the transcendence of the soul and its supplanting by an analytic deconstruction of the inner world. Just as the irruption of anatomical science marks the end of the body and death as metaphor and its entry on the scene as biological reality and fatality. I write 'entry on the scene' advisedly – the scene of objective truth, where the *confusion by default* between the human and inhuman, the living and the non-living, sex and the unsexed is played out. Whereas on the other scene – the scene of illusion and of forms – which is radically different from that of objective truth, is played out *the transfiguration by excess* of the human by the inhuman, of the living by the non-living, of sex by the unsexed.

The original, Enlightenment humanism was based on man's qualities, his virtues, his natural gifts, his essence, together with his right to freedom and to the exercise of that freedom. Current humanism, which finds its highest expression in the new extension of human rights, is more concerned with the conservation of the individual and of man as a species (in the one case, immortality is a virtue; in the other, it is merely a right to conservation). But human rights immediately become problematic, since the question arises of the potential rights of other species, of nature, etc., in respect of which they have to be defined. Now, does humanity even have rights over its own genome? What does it mean for a species to have the right to its

own genetic definition, and thus to its potential genetic transformation? We share 98 per cent of our genes with the apes, 90
per cent with mice. What rights attach to this common heritage?
On the other hand, it seems that 90 per cent of the human
genome is of no account. Are we going to claim this obscure part
which has no apparent purpose? As soon as the human is no
longer defined in terms of freedom and transcendence but in
terms of genes, the definition of man – and hence, also, that of
humanism – is wiped away.

The demarcation line of the human becomes increasingly
elusive as we press on into the biological realm, into the
molecular arcana of the biosphere. While Western humanism has
felt threatened since the sixteenth century by other cultures
bursting in upon it, the bolt currently giving way is no longer
merely that of a culture, but of a species. Anthropological
deregulation. And a simultaneous deregulation of ethics, of all the
moral, juridical, symbolic rules which were those of humanism.

The virtual transcendence of man, as distinct from his mortal
body, evaporates with the advance of genetic engineering.
Determination (or rather indeterminacy) becomes immanent in
the mapping of the genome, and its manipulation. Can we still
speak of souls and consciousness in referring to the automata,
chimeras and clones we envisage carrying on the human species?
Can we even speak of the unconscious, given the prospect of man
coming to be defined genetically? Even the immortality of the
unconscious, so dear to Freud, is seriously under threat. Not only
the individual, ontogenetic capital, but the phylogenetic capital of
the species is threatened by the evaporation of the limits of the
human, which is no longer an evaporation into the divine, but
into the inhuman and, indeed, not even into the inhuman but into
something falling short both of the human and the inhuman – the
genetic simulation of living beings.

The gods, the soul and immortality, all those things which have
been termed superstitions or fetishism, were still a spiritual,
metaphorical extrapolation of man's faculties, including the body
as a metaphor of resurrection. They were, admittedly, artifacts,
but immaterial ones, and ones which retained a projective force,

along with the power and play of illusion. Whereas, with biology and genetics, we are in pure materiality, in the material simulation of objectively immortal beings, since they are made up of nuclear elements and a timeless genetic code. The artificiality is no longer that of a deferred end, but of a prosthesis – a *literal* fetishism, in the sense that it is the fetishism of the literalness of the same and its reproduction. We are no longer dealing with an imaginary prosthesis, with the superstition of a supra-temporal soul, but with a material prosthesis – a simulation much more destructive than the illusion of the soul.

Moreover, the very illusion of the body, the play of appearances of the body, is destroyed in the simulation of the functions of life; appearances are volatilized by genetic transcription. Another vital illusion disappears: that of thought, which is abolished in the instrumentalization of mental faculties, in the fetishism of artificial intelligence.

There are several forms of death: a differentiated, dual, tragic form in the destiny of the higher mammals, which is linked to sexuality – in a way, a sexed form of death. And there is the asexual, undifferentiated form – a recessive stage which harks back to the molecular and protozoan stage of living beings, to their unceremonious obliteration, leaving them no other form of destiny.

In the concentration camps, even more than life, it was death that was exterminated. The prisoners were dispossessed of their deaths – deader than dead, disappeared. But death can also be exterminated by the creation of *indestructible life-processes*. Which is what we are doing when we attempt to capture immortality in anatomical, biological and genetic processes. Locked into their undifferentiated forms, either by the definitive autonomization of multiple functions or by reduction to the smallest possible elements, the life processes become indestructible, and it is by the automatic working of these processes that we are exterminating death by easy stages.

It was with this form of immortal life, this nostalgia for a pure contiguity of life [*le vivant*] and its molecular sequentiality, that Freud associated the death instinct. And it is to this kind of immortality that we are condemned today, as we are condemned to an absence of destiny, to the negative immortality of what cannot end and thus reproduces itself indefinitely.

In the past, man thought himself immortal, but he was not. Or rather he secretly doubted that he was not. Otherwise, he would not have needed to believe it. Today, we no longer believe we are immortal, yet it is precisely now that we are becoming so, becoming quietly immortal without knowing it, without wishing it, without believing it, by the mere fact of the confusion of the limits of life and death. No longer immortal in terms of the soul, which has disappeared, nor even in terms of the body, which is disappearing, but in terms of the formula, immortal in terms of the code. That is, we are beings for whom there will soon no longer be death, nor representation of death, nor even – and this is the worst – illusion of death.

In its classical, glorious sense, immortality is the quality of what passes beyond death, the quality of the supra-living. In its contemporary version, it is the quality of the sur-viving, that is, of what is already dead and, by that token, becomes immortal, but not at all in the same way. It is no longer a fateful attribute; it is the banal attribute of what is no longer threatened with death since it is already dead. Of what no longer comes to an end since it has already passed beyond its own ends, beyond its possibilities, into hypertely, so to speak, or into a 'surpassed' coma.

That immortality is the worst of fates, for death was the finest of man's conquests – subjective, dramatized death, death ritualized and celebrated, sought after and desired: by death, man distinguishes himself from all the other living species endowed with a natural immortality which, indeed, they share with the gods, whose immortal form is, initially, an animal one.

The question is whether, beyond all vicissitudes of religion and matters spiritual, beyond all belief, we are not returning, by the extradition of death, to that basic immortality. Are we not going back, as a result of all our technologies, to a (clonal, metastatic) *de facto* eternity which was, formerly, the destiny of the inhuman? But this functional immortality, instead of occurring in a 'world beyond', which at least had the advantage of being *another world*, is happening in this world, our world, which has, consequently, become our 'world beyond'. The disappearance of the boundaries of the human and the inhuman, of the limits of life and death, has turned our world itself into a 'world beyond' – this time a definitive 'world beyond', since there is no alternative to it in a real world, since it *is* the real world. It has itself become the site of total superstition.

How can you jump over your shadow when you no longer have one?

This compulsive desire for immortality, for a definitive immortality, revolves around a strange madness – the mania for what has achieved its goal. The mania for identity – for saturation, completion, repletion. For perfection too. The lethal illusion of perfection: hence these objects from which wear-and-tear, death or ageing have been eradicated by technology. The compact disc. It doesn't wear out, even if you use it. Terrifying, this. It's as though you'd never used it. It's as though you didn't exist. If objects no longer grow old when you touch them, you must be dead.

There is no better way of illustrating this madness than ironically, by the story of the man walking in the rain with his umbrella under his arm. When asked why he doesn't open it, he replies: 'I don't like to feel I've called on all my resources.' This says it all. Calling on all your resources is completely wrong-headed. To do so is to achieve immortality, but the immortality of the totalization, addition and repetition of yourself. Paradoxically, calling on all your resources is the opposite of knowing how to come to an end. To reach your own limits is no longer to have the end at your command. It means the abolition of death as vital horizon. It means losing your shadow. And so it means the impossibility of jumping over that shadow – how can you jump over your shadow when you no longer have one? In other words, if you want to live, you must not call on all your resources.

Yet this is the ideal everywhere set before us today, by way of the techniques of self-maximization, of performance blackmailing, of absolute realization of the human being as programme. The programming of all the genetic, biological, professional, existential variants of the individual. Going to the end of the programme, to the end of the tape! This way you arrive at a *de facto* immortality merely by forgetting the formula for stopping. Horizontal immortality, by acceleration and inertia, by exhaustion of possibilities, with the vertical cut-off of death no longer intervening. Even more illusory than all the transcendent forms of immortality, since it exhibits all the signs of material efficacy.

Yet nature provides us with an opposite example by leaving two-thirds of the human genome to lie fallow. One wonders what purpose these useless genes might serve, and why they should be forcibly decoded. What if they were only there to meet a requirement for a degree of leeway? If all the genes were functional, nothing would be wasted and we should be close to a total definition. It is perhaps to avert such a catastrophe that nature has provided this shadowy area. The same goes for language: the mass of floating signifier is what preserves language from calling on all its resources, which in turn preserves human beings from expressing everything and the world from signifying everything, from signifying in its totality. Yet this is precisely the aim today with computer technology, artificial intelligence, etc.: mobilizing all the neurons, all possible senses, and simultaneously reducing all margins, all the interstitial spaces. The trend in physics itself is towards the reduction of this interstitial void. It is the dream of that science to render matter totally concrete, to wrest all its energy from it by impelling it to limit-densities, densities artificial and monstrous.

What is it all about, then, this business of going as far as you can, exploiting all your resources, reaching your limits? It is a fantasy of death which leaves only the alternative of downfall and collapse. It is a strategy for wretches, for those who have so few means they are forced to exploit them to the full. It is a policy of self-exploitation one would never accept if it were imposed by someone else. It means cultivating servitude without the presence of the other, since each person substitutes himself for the other in the role of oppressor. The pinnacle of self-inflicted servitude. What will preserve us from this unlimited frenzy, this desire to abolish the horizon as perpetual line of flight, as virtual line of flight, which must remain virtual, but which we are precisely crossing today – towards that 'event horizon' beyond which nothing happens, nothing has meaning any longer and whence not even light escapes?

The intellectual field also functions like a system of crop-rotation, with ground left untilled, fallow. It has a mortal dread of developing all its faculties. Thought is precisely what puts a brake on ideas, which, left to themselves, tend to spread out uncontrolled and occupy the whole of space. Ideas proliferate like polyps or seaweed and perish by suffocating in their own luxuriant vegetation. There is an idea horizon just as there is an event horizon: the horizon of their death-dealing accomplishment, their absolute realization. Thought, for its part, leaks out into the void.

History too has called on all its resources. That is why it can now only turn around or repeat itself. It has not managed to leak out into the void. That is why it has become interminable, leaving scope only for a negative immortality.

The same goes for the social: we have attempted to mine the entire social sphere, to express it all, extort it all – we have tried to *realize* it by stripping it of any metaphorical dimension. This was to kill it by effusion, by diluting it into the real, by snuffing out its idea in the real.

It is, invariably, totally wrongheaded to attain the real – *real* immortality, the reality of the social. The end of metaphor, the absolute realization of all metaphors invariably marks the twilight of the idea and the refusal of death in death-dealing accomplishment.

A striking illustration of this killing of metaphors, dreams, illusions and utopias by their absolute realization, and of all ideas and transcendence by their material effectuation is provided by Canetti, who cites the example of the atomic bomb. He writes that, with Hiroshima and the dropping of the bomb, men put an end to the sun by harnessing its energy and materializing it on earth. They put an end to the illusion of the sun and its myth by mimicking the violence of its light and materializing it on earth in its radical form.*

The real is, in fact, the last resource of metaphor, but that resource must not be called on – on pain of death, on pain of losing its metaphorical power, its power of illusion. As in history, you have to keep your umbrella under your arm – a metaphor for the last chance – and not open it on any account. 'Every ecstasy ultimately prefers to take the path of renunciation rather than sin against its own concept by realizing itself' (Adorno).

One of the aspects of this mania for accomplishment is the elevation to the universal, which is commonly regarded as progress, as constituting in a way the extensional equivalent of immortality. This extension actually amounts to a dilution and extenuation of values in the universal. The same goes for events: it is when they are disseminated worldwide that their intensity is at its weakest and they are most rapidly obsolescent. The universalization of facts, data, knowledge, information is a precondition of their disappearance. Every idea and culture becomes universalized before it disappears. As with stars: their maximum expansion comes at the point of death, their transformation into red giants and then black dwarfs. The death agony of concentrated solutions in high dilution, the death agony of forms and images in high definition. This ending of cultures is not

* The Canetti passage to which Baudrillard is referring can be found in *The Human Province*, trans. Joachim Neugroschel. London: Deutsch, 1985, pp. 66–7.

perceptible from within. From within, a culture is immortal; it seems to approach its end only in an asymptotic curve. It has, in fact, already disappeared. The elevation of a value to universality is a prelude to its becoming transparent, which itself is a prelude to its disappearance.

There is no point, then, aiming for the universal, no point aiming for the heights, since there are no more heights. Erosion has done its work. If there is no longer any possibility of a philosophy of transcendence, since thought has been exiled to the other side of the looking-glass, there is no longer any possibility of conquering power either, since the political has been exiled to the other side of representation. There are no longer any heights to storm, either in the political domain or anywhere else, and the single-handed ocean crossings, which are our modern equivalent of climbing Annapurna, are posthumous fantasies.

This is the same impossibility as that of jumping over your shadow when you don't have one. It's a metaphysical leap which is beyond us. Peter Schlemihl had at least sold his shadow to the devil; ours we have simply lost. This is because we have, in the meantime, become entirely transparent. Or because there is not even a source of light, a bright enough energy source, to give us a shadow. Our only shadow is the one projected onto the wall opposite by atomic radiation. These stencilled silhouettes produced by the Hiroshima bomb. The atomic shadow, the only one left to us: not the sun's shadow, nor even the shadows of Plato's cave, but the shadow of the absent, irradiated body, the delineation of the subject's annihilation, of the disappearance of the original.

Another form of this identity mania is our contemporary individualism.

Neo-individualism, bent on performance and entrepreneurial heroism, athletic individualism (Alain Ehrenberg) – possibly neo-hedonistic, syncretic and tribal – bears no relation to the hero of bourgeois individualism. This latter, the hero of subjectivity, of breaking with the old, of free will and Stirner's radical singularity, is well and truly dead. Even Riesman's 'self-directed' individuality has disappeared from the horizon of the social as it has from the purview of the human sciences. The neo-individual is, by contrast, the purest product of 'other-directedness': an interactive, communicational particle, plugged into the network, getting continuous feedback, and with a clear vision of the podium in his mind's eye. Everyone is ready to turn themselves, depending on their various advantages or handicaps, into an autonomous micro-particle. And why not? This is the age of the daily invention of new particles. Why should the innumerable particles of our society not each demand their own identity and personal 'charm'? Obviously, this gives rise to chaotic sets and Brownian motion, in which freedom is merely the statistical end-product of impacts between singularities and no longer, therefore, in any sense a philosophical problem.

This individual is not an individual at all. He is a *pentito* of subjectivity and alienation, of the heroic appropriation of himself. His only aim is the technical appropriation of the self. He is a convert to the sacrificial religion of performance, efficiency, stress and time-pressure – a much fiercer liturgy than that of production – total mortification and unremitting sacrifice to the divinities of data [*l'information*], total exploitation of oneself by oneself, the ultimate in alienation.

No religion has ever demanded as much of the individual as such, and it might be said that radical individualism is the very form of religious integrism.* The modern religion of self-abnegation, of all-out operationality – the worst one of all since it recoups all the energy of irreligion, all the energy released by the eclipsing of traditional religions. This is the greatest irreligious conversion in history. By comparison with this voluntary holocaust, this escalation of sacrifice, the so-called return of religion which we pretend to fear – these occasional upsurges of religiosity or traditional integrism – is negligible. It merely conceals the fundamental integrism of this consensual society, the

---

* For reasons of context, this expression is used to render the French '*intégrisme religieux*' which, in other circumstances, might quite properly be translated as 'religious fundamentalism'.

terroristic fundamentalism of this new sacrificial religion of performance. It masks the fact that society as a whole is moving towards religious metastasis. Religious effects are taken too seriously in their religious dimension and not seriously enough as effects, that is, as masking the true process. This is a screen tumour, a fixation abscess which, by focusing it, allows the evil to be exorcized at little cost, sparing the need to analyse the whole society, to analyse 'democratic' society, which is virtually converted to integrism and revisionism, to security and protectionism and, at the same time, to the techniques of crude promotion and intimidation.

This 'post-modern' individualism arises not out of a problematic of *liberty* and *liberation*, but out of a *liberalization* of slave networks and circuits, that is, an individual diffraction of the programmed ensembles, a metamorphosis of the macro-structures into innumerable particles which bear within them all the stigmata of the networks and circuits – each one forming its own micro-network and micro-circuit, each one reviving for itself, in its micro-universe, the now useless totalitarianism of the whole.

In any case, in all registers – sex, culture, the economy, the media, politics – the concepts of liberty and liberation are diametrically opposed, unconditional liberation being the surest way of keeping liberty at bay. Liberty operates in a field that is limited and transcendent, in the symbolic space of the subject, where he is confronted with his own finality, his own destiny, whereas liberation operates in a potentially unlimited space. It is a quasi-physical process (its prototype is the liberation or release of energy) which pushes every function, every force, every individual to the limit of its possibilities and even beyond, where it is no longer answerable for its own actions. That is why liberty is a critical form, whereas liberation is a potentially catastrophic form. The former confronts the subject with his own alienation and its overcoming. The other leads to metastases, chain reactions, the disconnection of all elements and, finally, the radical expropriation of the subject. Liberation is the effective realization of the metaphor of liberty and, in this sense, it is also its end. There is no resolving the dilemma posed by these two. But the present system has found the final solution to both – in liberalization. Not the free subject any longer, but the liberal individual. No longer the liberation, but the liberalization of exchanges. From liberty to liberation, from liberation to liberalization. The extreme point of highest dilution, minimal intensity, where the problem of liberty cannot even be posed any longer.

And, in the process, the concept of alienation disappears. This new, cloned, metastatic, interactive individual is not alienated any longer, but self-identical. *He no longer differs from himself* and is, therefore, indifferent to himself. This indifference to oneself is at the heart of the more general problem of the indifference of institutions or of the political [*le politique*], etc., to themselves.

The indifference of time: the non-distance between points in time, the promiscuity of points in time, the instantaneousness of real time. Boredom.

The indifference of space: the televisual, remote-controlled contiguity and contamination of all points in space, which leaves you nowhere.

Political indifference: the superimposition, the proliferation of all opinions in a single media continuum.

Sexual indifference: indistinguishability and substitution of sexes as a necessary consequence of the modern theory of sex as difference.

The individual's indifference to himself and to others is a mirror-image of all these other kinds of indifference: it results from the absence of division within the subject, the suppression of the pole of otherness, from the subject's being inscribed in the order of identity, which is a product, paradoxically, of the demand that he be different from himself and from others.

For this identitary individual lives on the hymning and hallucinating of difference, employing to that end all the devices for simulating the other. He is the first victim of that psychological and philosophical theory of difference which, in all spheres, ends in indifference to oneself and others.

Difference is the infantile disorder of the subject (of our culture in general) and identity mania (the de-differentiation of self, indifference to self) is its senile disorder. We have conquered otherness with difference and, in its turn, difference has succumbed to the logic of the same and of indifference. We have conquered otherness with alienation (the subject becomes its own other), but alienation has, in its turn, succumbed to identity logic (the subject becomes the same as itself). And we have entered the interactive, sidereal era of boredom.

This identity syndrome has a particular form of madness specific to it. To the 'free' individual, the divided subject, there corresponds the vertical madness of yesteryear: psychical madness, the transcendent madness of the schizophrenic, that of alienation, of the inexorable transparence of otherness. To the identitary individual, that virtual clone, there corresponds a *horizontal* madness, our specific delirium and that of our whole culture: the delirium of genetic confusion, of the scrambling of codes and networks, of biological and molecular anomalies, of autism. No longer deliria of self-impairment or expropriation, but a delirium of self-appropriation – all the monstrous variants of identity – the delirium not of the schizophrenic but of the isophrenic, without shadow, other, transcendence or image – that of the mental isomorph, the autist who has, as it were, devoured his double and absorbed his twin brother (being a twin is, conversely, a form of autism *à deux*). Identitary, ipsomaniacal, isophrenic madness. Our monsters are all manic autists. As products of a chimerical combination (even where this is genetic), deprived of hereditary otherness, afflicted with hereditary sterility, they have no other destiny than desperately to seek out an otherness by eliminating all the Others one by one (whereas 'vertical' madness suffered, by contrast, from a dizzying excess of otherness). The problem of Frankenstein, for example, is that he has no Other and craves otherness. This is the problem of racism. But our computers also crave otherness. They are autistic, bachelor machines: the source of their suffering and the cause of their vengeance is the fiercely tautological nature of their own language.

Exponential instability, exponential stability

The whole problem of speaking about the end (particularly the end of history) is that you have to speak of what lies beyond the end and also, at the same time, of the impossibility of ending. This paradox is produced by the fact that in a non-linear, non-Euclidean space of history the end cannot be located. The end is, in fact, only conceivable in a logical order of causality and continuity. Now, it is events themselves which, by their artificial production, their programmed occurrence or the anticipation of their effects – not to mention their transfiguration in the media – are suppressing the cause–effect relation and hence all historical continuity.

This distortion of causes and effects, this mysterious autonomy of effects, this cause–effect reversibility, engendering a disorder or chaotic order (precisely our current situation: a reversibility of reality [*le réel*] and information, which gives rise to disorder in the realm of events and an extravagance of media effects), puts one in mind, to some extent, of Chaos Theory and the disproportion between the beating of a butterfly's wings and the hurricane this unleashes on the other side of the world. It also calls to mind Jacques Benveniste's paradoxical hypothesis of the memory of water. This latter becomes fascinating when we draw the parallels with our present world: through the extension of media and the means of communication, we too inhabit a highly diluted social and cultural universe in which the original molecules are increasingly rare. It would be interesting to know whether, in the human order too, effects persist in the absence of causes, whether a nominal substance remains active in the absence of its elements or even whether something can exist apart from any origin and reference. This is the problem of a logic of effects which is different from that of causes or perhaps simply of another causality than that of substances and forces – of an efficient causality of forms (some strange attractor?) out of all proportion with normal causal efficacy, and equivalent to the virtual efficacy of absent molecules. In this sense, we should no longer have to look for new energies in the material unleashing of substances but in the unconditional sequencing of forms.

Perhaps history itself has to be regarded as a chaotic formation, in which acceleration puts an end to linearity and the turbulence created by acceleration deflects history definitively from its end, just as such turbulence distances effects from their causes. We shall not reach the destination, even if that destination is the Last Judgement, since we are henceforth separated from it by a variable refraction hyperspace. The retroversion of history could very well be interpreted as a turbulence of this kind, due to the hastening of events which reverses and swallows up their course. This is one of the versions of Chaos Theory – that of *exponential instability* and its uncontrollable effects. It accounts very well for the 'end' of history, interrupted in its linear or dialectical movement by that catastrophic singularity which expresses itself in the exceptional form taken by contemporary events: these are both dramatic and insignificant, impatient to occur and indifferent to themselves (and to all of us). And it accounts, at the same time, for the impossibility of being done with history.

But the exponential instability version is not the only one. The other is that of *exponential stability*. This latter defines a state in which, no matter where you start out, you always end up at the same point. The initial conditions, the original singularities do not matter: everything tends towards the Zero point – itself also a strange attractor. None of the potentialities develops, whereas in exponential instability they extrapolate demonically. In exponential stability, there is therefore no end, not from effects becoming excessive and unpredictable, but because everything is already there, everything has already taken place.

We are thus immortal survivors, since the second existence is without end. It has no end because the end is already in the beginning. This is, therefore, a paradoxical immortality. 'The bomb exploded long ago, at Hiroshima. The process of dehumanization is complete and the clear effect of this phenomenon is that we no longer possess the psychical, ethical and spiritual resources which would enable us to realize this fact' (Romain Gary).

Though incompatible, the two hypotheses – exponential instability and stability – are in fact simultaneously valid. Moreover, our system, in its *normal* – normally catastrophic – course combines them very well. It combines in effect an inflation, a galloping acceleration, a dizzying whirl of mobility, an eccentricity of events and an excess of meaning and information with an exponential tendency towards total entropy. Our systems are thus doubly chaotic: they operate both by exponential stability and instability.

It would seem then that there will be no end because we are already in an excess of ends: the transfinite. And in an exceeding of finalities: transfinality. It is this excess which creates endless turbulence, indeed an involution and spiral disaggregation of time and history.

A disturbance is not, however, necessarily enigmatic. Sensitivity to initial conditions (Cleopatra's nose or the beating of a butterfly's wings) should not be confused, on the grounds that they are both incalculable, with fate or predestination. Indeed, precisely the opposite might be said to be true, insofar as predestination is, much rather, a *hypersensitivity to the final conditions* of a process, not to the initial ones. This is what makes a fateful – and not simply a chaotic or unpredictable –

configuration. In predestination, the end is there before the beginning and every effort to move away from the end brings that end closer: this is why it is tragic and ironic in character, and not merely eccentric or catastrophic, as in the patterns of chaos. Meteorology is chaotic; it is not a figure of destiny. All the extreme phenomena, the exorbitant effects, the vertiginous forms of disorder, everything which attests to the precession of effects over causes is fascinating, but not spiritually enthralling (and, here, we should have to include in the same order of forms the precession of models over the real, a phenomenon which encapsulates our modern 'destiny', the destiny of simulation which one may, in effect, read as a form of catastrophe of reality, this dizzying whirl of the model, the virtual and simulation carrying us further and further from the initial conditions of the real world). It is a logic of perverse effects (though some of these are beneficial), but it has nothing of a fatal strategy about it, since this latter requires a secret, but contradictory, will and a presentiment of total reversibility.

Chaos is a parody of any metaphysics of destiny. It is not even an avatar of such a metaphysics. The poetry of initial conditions fascinates us today, now that we no longer possess a vision of final conditions, and Chaos stands in for us as a negative destiny. The strangeness of the strange attractor is merely a metaphor; the radical strangeness lies in the enigmatic duality of a world and in the inexorable contradiction (that of our will and its loss) which keeps up the indestructible illusion. *Destiny is the ecstatic figure of necessity. Chaos is merely the metastatic figure of Chance.* Chaotic processes are random and statistical in nature and, even if they culminate in the hidden order of strange attractors, that still has nothing to do with the fulgurating notion of destiny, the absence of which is cruelly felt. It could even, no doubt, be said that only when destiny is absent do things begin to proliferate in all directions, only when there is no fateful resolution do the random equations of Chaos proliferate.

Our complex, metastatic, viral systems, condemned to the exponential dimension alone (be it that of exponential stability or instability), to eccentricity and indefinite fractal scissiparity, can no longer come to an end. Condemned to an intense metabolism, to an intense internal metastasis, they become exhausted within themselves and no longer have any destination, any end, any otherness, any fatality. They are condemned, precisely, to the epidemic, to the endless excrescences of the fractal and not to the reversibility and perfect resolution of the fateful [*fatal*]. We know only the signs of catastrophe now; we no longer know the signs of destiny. (And besides, has any concern been shown in Chaos Theory for the equally extraordinary, contrary phenomenon of *hyposensitivity* to initial conditions, of the inverse exponentiality of effects in relation to causes – the potential hurricanes which end in the beating of a butterfly's wings?)

Hysteresis of the millennium

We are, self-evidently, entering upon a retroactive form of history, and all our ideas, philosophies and mental techniques are progressively adapting to that model. We may perhaps even see this as an adventure, since the disappearance of the end is in itself an original situation. It seems to be characteristic of our culture and our history, which cannot even manage to come to an end, and are, as a result, assured of an indefinite recurrence, a backhanded immortality. Up to now, immortality has been mainly that of the beyond, an immortality yet to come, but we are today inventing another kind in the here and now, an immortality of endings receding to infinity.

The situation is, perhaps, an original one, but clearly, so far as the final result is concerned, the game is already lost. We shall never experience the original chaos, the Big Bang: the file is closed on that; we weren't there. But, where the final moment is concerned – the Big Crumb – we might have some hope of seeing that. Some hope of enjoying the end, to make up for not being able to enjoy the origin. These are the only two interesting moments and, since we have been denied the first, we might as well put all our energies into accelerating the end, into hastening things to their definitive doom, which we could at least consume as spectacle. Just imagine the extraordinary good luck of the generation which would have the end of the world to itself. It is every bit as marvellous as being present at the beginning. But we came too late for the beginning. Only the end seemed to be within our means.

We had come close to this possibility with the atomic age. Alas, the balance of terror suspended the ultimate event, then postponed it for ever(?) and, now deterrence has succeeded, we have to get used to the idea that *there is no end any longer, there will no longer be any end*, that history itself has become interminable. Thus, when we speak of the 'end of history', the 'end of the political', the 'end of the social', the 'end of ideologies', none of this is true. The worst of it all is precisely that there will be no end to anything, and all these things will continue to unfold slowly, tediously, recurrently, in that hysteresis of everything which, like nails and hair, continues to grow after death. Because, at bottom, all these things are already dead and, rather than have a happy or tragic resolution, a destiny, we shall have a thwarted end, a homeopathic end, an end distilled into all the various metastases of the refusal of death. The metastases of all that resurfaces as history goes back over its own tracks in a compulsive desire for rehabilitation, as though with regard to some crime or other (a crime committed by us, but in spite of ourselves, a crime of the species against itself, by a process which is quickening with contemporary history, a crime of which universal waste, universal repentance and universal *ressentiment* are, today, the surest signs), a crime on which the file has to be reopened, which necessarily involves going back into the past, right back to origins if necessary, where, for want of being able to find a resolution of our destiny in the future, we seek a retrospective absolution. We absolutely have to know what went wrong at a certain point and, hence, explore all the vestiges of the path we have travelled, root through the dustbins of history, revive both the best and the worst in the vain hope of separating good from evil. To return to Canetti's hypothesis: we have to get back beyond a fateful demarcation line which, in history too, might separate the human from the inhuman, a line which we might be said to have thoughtlessly crossed, in the dizzying whirl of some liberation of the species or other. It seems as though, caught up in a collective panic over this blind spot at which we passed out of history and its ends (but what were those ends? all we know is that we passed beyond them without noticing), we are hurriedly trying to get into reverse, in order to escape this state of empty simulation. Trying to relocate the zone of reference, the earlier scene, the Euclidean space of history. Thus the events in Eastern Europe claimed to set in train the onward march of peoples once more and the democratic process. And the Gulf War sought to reopen the space of war, the space of a violence that could establish a new world order.

This is, in every case, a failure. This revival of vanished – or vanishing – forms, this attempt to escape the apocalypse of the virtual, is a utopian desire, the last of our utopian desires. The more we seek to rediscover the real and the referential, the more we sink into simulation, in this case a shameful and, at any event, hopeless simulation.

By analogy with illnesses, which are perhaps merely the reactivation of previous states (cancer, for example, reproducing the undifferentiated proliferation of the first living cells, or viral pathology, which causes the earlier states of the biogenetic substance to resurface in moments when the body is weak and its immune defences low), can we not imagine that, in history itself, previous states have never disappeared, but present themselves again in succession, as it were, taking advantage of the weakness or excessive complexity of the present structures?

However, these earlier forms never resurface as they were; they never escape the destiny of extreme modernity. Their resurrection is itself hyper-real. The resuscitated values are themselves fluid, unstable, subject to the same fluctuations as fashion or stock-exchange capital. The rehabilitation of the old frontiers, the old structures, the old elites will therefore never have the same meaning. If, one day, the aristocracy or royalty recover their old position, they will, nonetheless, be 'post-modern'. None of the 'retro' scenarios that are being got up has any historical significance: they are occurring wholly on the surface of *our* age, as though all images were being superimposed one upon another, but with no change to the actual course of the film. Relapsed events: defrosted democracy, *trompe-l'oeil* freedoms, the New World Order cellophane-wrapped and ecology in mothballs, with its immune-deficient human rights. None of these will make any difference to the *present* melancholy of the century, which we shall never get right through, since it will, in the meantime, have swung around and headed off in the opposite direction.

This is all, at bottom, a triumph for Walt Disney, that inspired precursor of a universe where all past or present forms meet in a playful promiscuity, where all cultures recur in a mosaic (including the cultures of the future, which are themselves already recurrent). For a long time we thought this was all imaginary, that is, derivative and decorative, puerile and marginal. But we are going to see that it was something like a prefiguration of the real trend of things – Disneyworld opening up for us the bewildering perspective of passing through all the earlier stages, as in a film, with those stages hypostasized in a definitive juvenility, frozen like Disney himself in liquid nitrogen: Magic Country, Future World, Gothic, Hollywood itself reconstituted fifty years on in Florida, the whole of the past and the future revisited as living simulation. Walt Disney is the true hero of deep-freezing, with his utopian hope of awakening one day in the future, in a better world. But that is where the irony bites: he had not foreseen that reality and history would turn right around. And he, who expected to wake up in the year 2100, might well, following out his own fairytale scenario, awaken in 1730 or the world of the Pharaohs or any one of his many primal scenes.

We wondered what the point of this coming *fin de siècle* might be. Here we have it: the sale of the century. History is being sold off, as is the end of history. Communism is being sold off, as is the end of communism. Communism will have had no historical end; it will have been sold off, knocked down like useless stock. Just like the Russian army, sold off at the four corners of the earth – an unprecedented event relegated to the status of a banal market operation. All Western ideologies are knocked down too; they can be had at bargain prices in all latitudes.

The sales used to come after the feast days but now they precede them. It's the same with our century: we are anticipating the end – everything must go, everything has to be sold off. We learn, for example, that, alongside the great Red Army stock clearance, the industrial laboratories are currently 'selling off' the human genome, which they are copyrighting and commercializing sequence by sequence. Here again, everything must go, even if we don't know what these genes are for. Things must not be allowed to reach their natural term. They have first to be cryogenized, in order to ensure them a virtual, derisory immortality.

Messianic hope was based on the *reality* of the Apocalypse. But this latter has no more reality than the original Big Bang. We shall never be allowed this dramatic illumination. Even the idea of putting an end to our planet by an atomic clash is futile and superfluous. If it has no meaning for anyone, God or man, then what is the point? Our Apocalypse is not real, it is *virtual*. And it is not in the future, it is *here and now*. Our orbital bombs, even if they did not mean a natural end, were at least manufactured by us, designed, as it seems, the better to end it all. But, in actual fact, that is not how it was: they were made *the better to be rid of the end*. We have now put that end into satellite form, like all those finalities which, once transcendent, have now become purely and simply orbital.

It circles around us, and will continue to do so tirelessly. We are encircled by our own end and incapable of getting it to land, of bringing it back to earth. This is like the parable of the Russian cosmonaut forgotten in space, with no one to welcome him, no one to bring him back – the sole particle of Soviet territory ironically overflying a deterritorialized Russia. Whereas on earth everything has changed, he becomes practically immortal and continues to circle like the gods, like the stars, like nuclear waste. Like so many events, of which he is the perfect illustration, which continue to circle in the empty space of news [*l'information*], without anyone being able or willing to bring them back into historical space. A perfect image of all those things which continue their uncompromising performance in orbit, but have lost their identity along the way. Our history, for example, has also got lost along the way and revolves around us like an artificial satellite.

Nostalgia for the lost object? Not even that. Nostalgia had beauty because it retained within it the presentiment of what has taken place and could take place again. It was as beautiful as utopia, of which it is the inverted mirror. It was beautiful for never being satisfied, as was utopia for never being achieved. The sublime reference to the origin in nostalgia is as beautiful as the reference to the end in utopia. It is something else again to be confronted with *the literal manifestness of the end* (of which we can no longer dream as end), and the literal manifestness of the origin (of which we can no longer dream as origin). Now, we have the means today to put into play both our origins and our end. We exhume our origins in archaeology, reshape our original capital through genetics, and operationalize our dreams and the wildest utopias by means of science and technology. We appease our nostalgia and our utopian desires *in situ* and *in vitro*.

We are, then, unable to dream of a past or future state of things. Things are in a state which is literally definitive – neither finished, nor infinite, nor definite, but de-finitive that is, deprived of its end. Now, the feeling which goes with a definitive state, even a paradisiac one – is melancholic. Whereas, with mourning, things come to an end and therefore enjoy a possibility of returning, with melancholia we are not even left with the presentiment of an end or of a return, but only with *ressentiment* at their disappearance. The crepuscular profile of the *fin de siècle* is more or less of this order, combining the features of a linear order of progress and a regression, itself also linear, of ends and values.

Against this general movement, there remains the completely improbable and, no doubt, unverifiable hypothesis of a *poetic reversibility of events*, more or less the only evidence for which is the existence of the same possibility in language.

The poetic form is not far removed from the chaotic form. Both flout the law of cause and effect. If, in Chaos Theory, for sensitivity to initial conditions we substitute sensitivity to final conditions, we are in the form of predestination, which is the form of fate [*le destin*]. Poetic language also lives with pre-destination, with the imminence of its own ending and of reversibility between the ending and the beginning. It is pre-destined in this sense – it is an unconditional event, without meaning and consequence, which draws its whole being from the dizzying whirl of final resolution.

It is certainly not the form of our present history and yet there is an affinity between the immanence of poetic development and the immanence of the chaotic development which is ours today, the unfolding of events which are themselves also without meaning and consequence and in which – with effects substituting themselves for causes – there are no longer any causes, *but only effects*. The world is there, *effectively*. There is no reason for this, and God is dead.

If nothing exists now but effects, we are in a state of total illusion (which is also that of poetic language). If the effect is in the cause or the beginning in the end, then the catastrophe is behind us. This reversing of the sign of catastrophe is the exceptional privilege of our age. It liberates us from any future catastrophe and any responsibility in that regard. The end of all anticipatory psychoses, all panic, all remorse! The lost object is behind us. We are free of the Last Judgement.

What this brings us to, more or less, is a poetic, ironic analysis of events. Against the simulation of a linear history 'in progress', we have to accord a privileged status to these backfires, these malign deviations, these lightweight catastrophes which cripple an empire much more effectively than any great upheavals. We have to accord a privileged status to all that has to do with non-linearity, reversibility, all that is of the order not of an unfolding or an evolution, but of a winding back, a reversion in time. Anastrophe versus catastrophe. Perhaps, deep down, history has never unfolded in a linear fashion; perhaps language has never unfolded in a linear fashion. Everything moves in loops, tropes, inversions of meaning, except in numerical and artificial languages which, for that very reason, *no longer are* languages. Everything occurs through effects which short-circuit their (metaleptic) causes, through the *Witze* of events, perverse events, ironic turnabouts, except within a rectified history, which, for just that reason, *is not* a history.

Might we not transpose language games on to social and historical phenomena: anagrams, acrostics, spoonerisms, rhyme, strophe and catastrophe? Not just the major figures of metaphor and metonymy, but the instant, puerile, formalistic games, the heteroclite tropes which are the delight of a vulgar imagination? Are there social spoonerisms, or an anagrammatic history (where meaning is dismembered and scattered to the winds, like the name of God in the anagram), rhyming forms of political action or events which can be read in either direction? In these times of a retroversion of history, the palindrome, that poetic, rigorous form of palinode, could serve as a *grille de lecture* (might it not perhaps be necessary to replace Paul Virilio's dromology with a palin-dromology?). And the anagram, that detailed process of un-ravelling, that sort of poetic and non-linear convulsion of language – is there a chance that history lends itself to such a poetic convulsion, to such a subtle form of return and anaphora which, like the anagram, would – beyond meaning – allow the pure materiality of language to show through, and – beyond historical meaning – allow the pure materiality of time to show through?

Such would be the enchanted alternative to the linearity of history, the poetic alternative to the disenchanted confusion, the chaotic profusion of present events.

In this very way, we enter, beyond history, upon pure fiction, upon the illusion of the world. The illusion of our history opens on to *the greatly more radical illusion of the world*. Now we have closed the eyelids of the Revolution, closed our eyes on the Revolution, now we have broken down the Wall of Shame, now that the lips of protest are closed (with the sugar of history which melts on the tongue), now Europe – and memories – are no longer haunted by the spectre of communism, nor even by that of power, now the aristocratic illusion of the origin and the democratic illusion of the end are increasingly receding, we no longer have the choice of advancing, of persevering in the present destruction, or of retreating – but only of facing up to this radical illusion.